THE SEARCH FOR TRUTH

LIFE CHANGING ANSWERS TO MANKIND'S TOUGHEST QUESTIONS

PAUL ELWELL

IUNIVERSE, INC.
NEW YORK   BLOOMINGTON

The Search for Truth
Life changing answers to mankind's toughest questions

iUniverse books may be ordered through booksellers or by contacting:

iUniverse
1663 Liberty Drive
Bloomington, IN 47403
www.iuniverse.com
1-800-Authors (1-800-288-4677)

Because of the dynamic nature of the Internet, any Web addresses or links contained in this book may have changed since publication and may no longer be valid.

ISBN: 978-1-4502-6106-7 (sc)
ISBN: 978-1-4502-6107-4 (ebk)

Library of Congress Control Number: 2010914134

Printed in the United States of America

iUniverse rev. date: 10/15/2010

CONTENTS

INTRODUCTION

I sat there in my chair feeling a little perplexed as the professor drew a picture on the chalkboard to illustrate his point. He turned back around and continued to lecture: "Morals, you see, are not the same to all people in all cultures. People living in a particular tribe in Africa may have a different moral code than you or I may have." As I pondered the implications of his statement, I soon began to think that they did not make much sense. He continued: "We should not try to legislate morality because morality varies among cultural groups and even between people. You may believe that something is right for you. The person to your right might believe something else is right for him. The person to your left might believe something else is right for her. In our American culture, we have been brainwashed in Sunday School with the Judaeo-Christian system of ethics. The truth, class, is that when it comes to ethics and morality one size does *not* fit all."

This professor was biased against anyone who held any type of religious views. He believed that Christianity was based entirely on myths and that the Bible had long ago been discredited as full of contradictions and errors. He proceeded to "expose" a philosophical error in the nature of the God presented in the Bible. He started by saying that the Bible teaches that God is omniscient, omnipotent and omnibenevolent (which means that God is all-knowing, all-powerful, and all-good). He stated: "If God is all of these things— all-knowing, all-powerful, and all good—then he can do anything. Well, then, can God murder? If he cannot then he is not all-powerful, and if he can then he is not all good."

He ranted on, proud of himself for "exposing" the absurdity of Christian theology: "Can God lie? Can God make a rock so big he can't lift it?" Although these arguments seemed absurd and rather childish, they struck me as containing a grain of truth. There *was* a logical problem, it seemed. I made the mistake of challenging him on this point after class. He discounted me as merely one more of those simple-minded crazy people who grew up in church and had never thought about philosophy and the real world. "The Bible is great for Sunday School lessons," he said, "but it can't withstand the tests of academia and philosophy." He told me that I was just taking the Bible's stories on "blind faith"; any true scholar knew that the Bible was merely an antiquated book of legends compiled by Jewish editors.

I left class that day feeling a little dejected, wondering: "What if what I have been taught all my life could not stand up to criticism or the tests of logical consistency?" I decided I would set out on a journey to answer life's toughest questions. I would hold the Bible up to the toughest tests of logic and science and see if it was internally coherent. I began both modern and classical philosophers, looking critically at the Bible's so-called "errors" and examining them to see if they were, in fact, errors. I wanted to know if the Bible truly was from God and concluded that, if it was, it should present a complete worldview capable of withstanding any tests and questions that philosophers, historians, and scientists could put to it. I proposed 10 questions:

Does absolute truth exist?

Are all belief systems based on "Blind Faith?"

How do you determine right and wrong?

Can man live without God?

Don't all religions lead to God?

Is there a God?

What is the meaning of life?

How do I know that I know?

How did I get here?

Why is there evil and suffering?

What happens after death?

I determined at the start of my search that if the Bible—and the Christian worldview derived from it—could not answer every one of these questions then it was not worth following. The book that follows is what I found....

DOES ABSOLUTE TRUTH EXIST?

Ding, dong, ding, dong. I heard the clock down stairs chime eight more times signaling it was midnight on a Friday night and, by the time, the clock stopped sounding, it was Saturday morning. I was home alone studying the topic of truth. More specifically, I sought the nature of truth and whether it really exists in a concrete form. My wife left me at home so I could have some quiet time to study and continue on my path to determine what I believed. I turned back to the book I was reading, which contained the writings and thoughts of many of the greatest philosophers the world has ever known. However, as I read, my mind seemed to drift back to one thing I had read earlier that night in the Bible. Pontius Pilate asked Jesus a question while he was on trial in John 18:38: "What is truth?" Philosophers, theologians, ethicists, most college students, and most thinking people have asked this question many times since. We all want to know, does truth exist? Moreover, we wonder the same question Pontius Pilate asked Jesus: "what is truth?" How do we determine what is true? Furthermore, is truth universal or does it depend upon my situation and/or cultural norms to determine what is true?

The more I read, the more I realized that people discuss and debate the topic of truth without ever coming to a solid conclusion of what they mean by the term. For example, once I was on an airplane flying back from Alaska to Chicago when a woman in her mid twenties sat down next to me. We began to chat about what we were doing in Alaska and so on. Eventually, in the conversation, her Jewish background came up. She told me she really enjoyed Judaism because the lessons taught in the synagogue were open to interpretation and many of the rabbis who had written about the Torah disagreed about its meaning. She went on to say this was nice because the religion was not cut-and-dried like other religions; there were many different ways to believe with no one set of rules. I listened intently as she explained how this made her feel good that her religious beliefs did not have some strict set of rules to follow; instead, things were flexible and open to each person's own interpretation. She did not realize that she was living a contradiction. I asked her if murder was wrong, to which she responded it was. I then asked her if there is no absolute source of truth regarding why it was wrong to murder. She said it was because of morals. Yet, she rejected the idea that there was any source of absolute truth. So, on the one hand, she believed in morality and that some things should not be done. On the other hand, she rejected all basis for these rules.

Before we can answer this fundamental question, we must first define our terms. *Absolute truth* is defined as *fixed, invariable, unalterable facts*. For example, it is absolutely true that every triangle has three sides; there can never be a four-sided triangle. Absolute truth is definite and unchanging. This is logically necessary because to deny truth is to claim truth. Thus, if you say, "Not every triangle has four sides," what you are really saying is "It is true that some triangles have more or fewer than three sides" (which is a statement of "truth"). This violates the Law of Non-Contradiction, which states that two contradictory statements cannot both be correct at the same time and in the same sense.

This law is often violated. Let us consider some examples. Have you ever heard someone say, "There is no such thing as truth" or "Truth is relative"? These statements cannot be logically correct. To assert that truth does not exist is a self-defeating statement because, after all, the statement itself is claiming to be truth. So the statement "There is no such thing as truth" really means that the only true statement is that "truth does not exist." But this very statement proves that truth exists. It is like trying to describe a one-ended stick—it cannot be done (because a stick by definition has two ends). When people argue that no truth exists, they are proving the very statement they have set out to disprove.

Another example is found in the declaration "Words have no meaning." The person who states this proves the very opposite of his claim. The phrase "Words have no meaning" actually expresses that words do, in fact, mean something. Otherwise, the statement is absurd. To honestly express that "Words have no meaning," you would need to communicate the meaning of the statement without using any words at all (written or spoken) because the very use of words proves the point the speaker is trying to disprove.

The most common assault against absolute truth is that "Truth is relative." What this means to say is that each individual has his own "truth" to live by or that "truth" varies depending on the situation. Sometimes it comes in a bold proclamation: "We can't know truth" or "What's true for you is not true for me." The speaker asks you to agree. This argument fails, though, because the statement "Everything is relative" (including truth) is relative to itself because, according to its "truth," that very statement is sometimes true to some people in some situations and sometimes untrue to other people in other situations.

Relativism—the belief that all truth is relative—always contradicts itself and makes no sense in the real world. For example, let's consider a person who murders a child in a relativist worldview. Believing that the world exists only for his pleasure, the murderer does whatever makes him the happiest. His actions are based solely on his personal truth that holds that the objective of his life is the pursuit of pleasure and doing what makes him feel good. He does not believe that murdering a child is wrong, even though another person—such as a Christian bound by the Bible's laws and restrictions—might believe that it is. Meanwhile society, witnessing the abuse and the trauma the child and the family suffers as a consequence, has no one to hold responsible for the damage unless it relies on an objective standard of truth by which to condemn the practice of killing children.

If truth is relative, the pleasure-seeking worldview of the murder is the final judge of right and wrong—what brings pleasure is right and what does not bring pleasure is wrong. We would have no right, therefore, to question his decision, no objective authority to appeal to because the murderer *believed* this action was right.

THE HUMBLE STOP SIGN

Do moral absolutes come from human consensus (e.g., government, prevailing public opinion, legislators) or from universal standards given by God? Human consensus can change. For example, prior to World War II most Americans believed Hitler was harmless. We now know that this prevailing public opinion was untrue. The majority can be wrong, and just because an idea is popular does not make it right in any absolute sense. Without a supreme ethic from God to judge right and wrong, we cannot judge any action as right or wrong.

The main complaint of the relativist is that others are trying to impose their worldview on him (i.e., "legislating morality"). All laws, however, are derived from a worldview imposed on the people subject to the law. The question is only *which* worldview will be imposed. For example, a stop sign and the law that prohibits running it are legislated morality. The sign says that those with the power to legislate morality (e.g., federal, state, and local lawmakers) believe property rights are important enough to impose on citizens because it is in the interests of society to prevent people from crashing into each other and damaging others' property. The sign also imposes a belief—and legislates the morality—that human life is valuable because it stops people from causing themselves and others' bodily injury.

Even something as simple as a stop sign imposes values and a worldview on everyone. There is not a single law on the books that does not impose a moral worldview. It is true that those who make the laws are imposing morality on others because any law imposes a worldview on those who are legally required to obey it.

If we follow relativism—the pleasure principle and the belief that no one has the right to impose a moral value on anyone else—to its logical conclusion, however, we see that a relativist worldview not only includes justification for the child molesters but murderers, rapists, and terrorists as well. If the worldview that truth is relative and doing what brings pleasure is the highest good, then they are justified in their actions when they molest, murder, rape, and plant bombs on school buses.

If we apply the Christian worldview to the situation, however, we have a supreme ethic given by God Himself shown in His character and revealed in His word, the Bible. His revelation in the Bible is the standard by which we judge right and wrong. He has provided us with an unchanging standard of truth to live by. If we impose this standard of truth on others, we help them by giving a standard that protects their life, property, and personal rights—rights given by God Himself. We can contrast this respect and protection of rights with the respect of the relativist as he imposes his ideas and worldview on everyone around him, which is ultimately respect only for his own desires.

The bottom line is that *truth is inescapable.* The more we attempt to disprove its existence, the more we find out its depth in human experience. Relativism violates the Law of Non-Contradiction because in this worldview, two people can do the same thing at the same time and one can be right and the other wrong. Relativism is the expression of everyone doing what is right in his or her own eyes. It is a moral paradigm that will always lead to social chaos, disaster, and death. To be fair, most relativists are "good people" who believe it is wrong to commit murder, rape, and other horrific crimes against others. They often add the caveat that anything is okay as long as it does not hurt anybody. However, an honest application of their worldview contradicts their moral beliefs. Their theory of life holds that the opposite view is equally valid.

For instance, one relativist thinks it is wrong to steal and another thinks it is OK to steal under some circumstances (say, underreporting taxes) and does so. Both views, according to the relativist, are valid. Neither relativist can say the other's view is wrong in any absolute sense. The only way a relativist can justify his position not to steal is to borrow from the Christian worldview and use it as a restraint against evil while still claiming that truth is relative. The Bible and the principles of morality within it give us a basis for determining right and wrong. The Bible gives the Christian a solid foundation upon which to base moral judgments. Many relativists do so in order to pursue personal indulgences that the Bible forbids. In the end, they reject the truth not based on logic but on the desire to pursue their own pleasures without hindrance from a God who holds them accountable. Our human nature, however, cannot escape the feeling that there is more to life than our current existence. We struggle to explain our current situation in the absence of a supernatural being.

We humans are designed to search for truth and meaning. Ideally, the search will lead us to the only ultimate source of truth—God. The bottom line is: We all have an innate desire to worship something. Left to themselves, humans will not become atheists. They will find *something* to worship in their attempt to find truth and meaning. History has proven that humanity will make up all sorts of things to worship in place of the one true God. Our own day is no different. While few have a statue of Zeus in their house, many people worship idols of the mind—such things as money, career, good deeds, physical appearance, pride, fame, other people, sports, academic endeavors, and power (to name but a few).

Sources claiming to have truth all fall short of providing knowable truth. These "truth sources" give us information, but they cannot give us a reliable standard of truth. Some examples of these are science, religious gurus, and logic. The only reliable source of truth available is someone who knows all, has seen all, and has created all things. Anything less is someone speaking about things they do not fully understand. As humans, we see things in perspective, which is limited, and not as they truly are. God has been everywhere, seen everything, and created all things, and therefore knows all things. He has graciously revealed His truth in the Bible, which we call His word—the revealed truth. As such, it is the only reliable, irrefutable, and infallible source of truth available to humanity. The Bible is the very word of God. It exposes humanity's problem: being separated from God. It reveals who God is, His nature, and the cure for our common problem of sin. The Bible shows us the only way to God and how we can be at peace with Him.

ARE ALL BELIEF SYSTEMS BASED ON "BLIND FAITH?"

Faith is a concept that is commonly misunderstood. I recall my college professor scoffing at the idea; calling any idea not tested by empirical means a matter of "blind faith" or something believed not on a logical basis, contrary to empirical evidence. He seemed quite proud not to have faith-based convictions (or so he thought) that were built on anything but logic and empirically verifiable evidence. As I thought about the idea of faith, I thought of the implications of faith. I knew the Bible said in Hebrews 11:6, "...without faith it is impossible to please God." Therefore, I knew that the Christian worldview required faith, but what does this mean? I pondered this question. Do we go into church and turn our brains off at the door? Are we not to think critically about the things we are taught or question what is being said? Do we just compartmentalize these things taught in church as "religious things" that we believe but deep down we know they are not true? The more I thought about faith I realized that faith is not believing what you know isn't true. That is insanity. This is similar to believing Santa Claus put the presents under the tree at Christmas time, despite catching your parents in the act.

The more I pondered the criticism the professor gave me, I came to see that he relied upon faith as much as I did. He could not prove his presuppositions; they had to be taken by faith as did mine. Therefore, no one can escape faith. We all have faith in something because we all have presuppositions, axioms or unproven starting points. Presuppositions, or unproven starting points, are the basis for logical thought. One of my professor's presuppositions, which he pretended did not exist, was that truth could be known entirely through empirical evaluation of the world around us. His pretence was wanting to argue based upon, in his mind, that nothing can be taken on faith. Of course, he disregarded the fact that he was taking his presupposition as true based on faith. He was essentially asking me to enter dialogue with him leaving my presuppositions behind, but all the while he was using presuppositions of his own. The fundamental nature of his invitation to debate was that I must not bring my presuppositions in the debate but his were the presuppositions I must agree to in order to debate with him. His presuppositions must be accepted based on faith, just as mine. This is because a presupposition is by definition an untested starting point.

What the professor had tried to do was to use his presuppositions but exclude all others. He automatically ruled out that a word from God could be an ultimate authority because it relies upon the Bible to authenticate the Word of God. He was essentially saying ultimate authorities cannot authenticate themselves but, for this to be true, nothing can be an ultimate authority including empirical evaluation. This is because every ultimate truth source authenticates itself in order to be an ultimate authority. If an ultimate truth source was able to be authenticated by another source it would no longer be an ultimate authority, because the source that authenticated it would be a superior source of truth.

There is no neutral ground when it comes to arguing truth. We both cannot put aside our presuppositions and argue from a point of neutrality because one does not exist. We must all have presuppositions in order for the world to make sense. If we truly had no presuppositions, we could not have carried on a logical conversation or had a meaningful debate. Instead, we would have both had to wonder what point the other was trying to make because we would have no basis to believe that the conclusion that flowed from the argument was legitimate. We instead both relied upon a source outside of the physical realm, which gives us laws of logic in which we can converse and debate.

This is the key turning point in the debate. We have no basis explainable by natural physical means to believe that if A=B and B=C than A=C. If logic is simply a set of conventions agreed to among men we must ask, "Do we use logic simply because it has always worked out?" If this is the case, then we would have no reason to believe that in the above example A will always equal C in the future. If it ever happened that A did not equal C, then all logical ideas would have to be redeveloped. Furthermore, we would have no reason to believe that A would always equal C tomorrow. The laws of logic could change and A would not equal C; everything we understood about the world would become false.

We accept the laws of logic because we have a God who has created the world and put them in place in order to give us a meaningful way to communicate and understand the world around us. The more we study logic and the world around us, the more we understand that the Bible is correct that "The fear of the Lord is the beginning of knowledge" Proverbs 1:7 . Therefore, we must start with the Bible in order to have a basis to understand the world around us. One may ask, "if this is true, then why can the person who rejects God still use logical ideas, communicate with others, and be able to use the laws of logic in their daily life?" This is a very good point. Christians do not have a monopoly on logic simply because they have the only means by which it can be explained. This is part of God's common grace that He has given everyone the ability to think logically and communicate in a logical manner with those around them. The key thing is that the person who rejects God has to borrow the Christian worldview in order to try to refute the Christian worldview. Cornelius Van Til illustrated this by saying "You must sit on your father's lap in order to slap him in the face." (Geehan, 1971) This is what the non-Christian is doing. They use the God-given ability to think logically to debate, trying to prove that there is no God. All the while, they fail to understand they must assume what they reject in order to argue against what they have already assumed.

Why would someone do this? Is it a lack of knowledge? No. Some of the most notable atheists are brilliant men. Many hold advanced degrees and are brilliant philosophers. However, they reject the foundation on which they then turn around and use to fight the truth. This is because facts do not change people's minds. Banshen illustrates this point well in the following story. A man was seeing a psychologist because he had a strange belief that he was dead. The psychologist argued with him and tried to convince him that this was obviously untrue, but to no avail. Despite the best efforts of the psychologist, the man still believed he was dead. Finally, exasperated, the psychologist asked the man if dead men bleed. The man replied, "No, dead men do not bleed." Having received the confirmation he was looking for, the psychologist reached over to the man and stabbed him with his pen, causing blood to flow. The psychologist then said "see, you bleed; so you are not dead." The man had an astonished look on his face and said in shock, "I guess dead men do bleed." (Bahnsen, March 2007).

You see, as is illustrated in this humorous example, we all have beliefs that we hold at different levels. We may hold some beliefs at very high level, such as my belief that the Detroit Tigers are going to win the World Series next year. If this does not come true, not much is lost. However, we hold other beliefs at a lower level such as our beliefs of the truth or the possibility, or lack thereof, of the supernatural. When one of our beliefs is proven to be untrue, we filter the new information we come to know through the lens of our lower level or more foundational level beliefs. Therefore, when someone holds as a foundation level belief that there is no god, then, even if logically proven to them, this new evidence is filtered through the lens of the more foundational belief and then reinterpreted. This is why I say that facts do not change people's minds. Only a change of their foundational level beliefs change people's minds. I can prove that the non-Christian worldview leads to a life of contradiction and, if lived consistently, insanity. However, this will not change the mind of those who hold more foundational level beliefs that are not consistent with what they are being shown.

You may wonder why I say if the non-Christian worldview is lived constantly, it leads to insanity. Let me explain. While many people bow to the presupposition that there is no God, or outright reject the possibility of the super natural, few actually view the world in a way consistent with their belief system. Those who try to live a life consistent with the logical implications of a life without God find the horrific consequences of this choice. First, there is no standard of authority to govern behavior or any ethical standard to which one can hold himself or others, beyond arbitrary individualistic standards of conduct. Secondly, there is no basis for logic. This is critical and devastating because there are only two choices for the origin and source of the laws of logic. One is that it is a human convention among men, which we all agree to follow because it seems to work every time we test it empirically. The problem with this is that, if this is true, we base the laws of logic on past experience. We have no assurance that what we experience in the past will hold true for the future. This means those who claim this view would say, because a logical test proved itself true in the past and it proves itself true in the present, we believe in the future events that happen in the future past will be true in the future present. However, this is not logically possible to prove. They actually have no logical basis to believe that events in the future past will hold true in the future present. Those who want to live consistently with their beliefs will find this the hardest to follow. The reason is that, in order to be consistent, one must reject logic and embrace insanity. Let me explain. Once you realize that you have no logical basis for the future past to be the same as the future present, you then realize you have no basis to believe the present will be as the past has been; there is no basis for logical thought whatsoever. For example, if one wanted to be consistent and realized that logically the worldview requires one to reject logic, they can no longer have a basis for understanding why two words or two sentences put together make sense. Furthermore, one cannot understand why, if they touched a hot stove and it hurt the first time, it would not feel good the second time they placed their hand on that same hot stove. All of these things require logical inference, which a non-believer has no basis for anymore. Thus, the two options open to the person who rejects God are:

1. Live inconsistently with your beliefs and borrow the Christian worldview in order to reason.
2. Reject logic and embrace insanity.

These may not appeal to those who reject God as the source of truth and the final authority but their own worldview leaves them no other options. In the end, God has built this world and given to us the laws of logic, in which, we can make sense of the world around us. He has left this as evidence of his existence and creative power, which testifies of Him. In order to function in our world, one must use the God-given Christian worldview. This leaves everyone without an excuse. They either accept Him as God or knowingly and willfully reject the God who has shown Himself to them and offered them the gift of salvation.

How do you determine right and wrong?

From the very beginning, humanity has struggled with the question of how to determine right and wrong. Many questions arise about why we naturally think some things are right and others are wrong. Our inherent conscience tells us, through feelings of guilt and shame, that certain actions are wrong. But where did this inner voice come from, and why do people still commit evil acts in violation of their conscience?

Conscience as a Guide

Let us look at an extreme example: a serial killer. He was not a "natural born" killer, but by constantly ignoring his internal moral compass, his conscience became callused. Continuing down this path, he was capable of doing whatever evil he desired without remorse. He silenced and ignored his conscience for so long that he could no longer feel its pangs. We cannot say, however, that he was "free" from the bonds of conscience because the freedom that the serial killer feels (or that anyone else feels) once he has ignored his conscience for so long is not really freedom at all—it is bondage. It is like being a fish out of water. The fish is not free from the water; the fish out of water is really dying. The water is there for the fish's good and his survival, not to limit or restrict him.

Our conscience is within us to be our guide for survival in life. Listening to our conscience restrains us from acting out all the evil impulses that are naturally within our hearts. For example, have you ever had a thought that if acted upon would have had horrible consequences? I know I have. I am glad that I do not act on everything that comes into my mind. The heart of man is "desperately wicked" (Jeremiah 17:9) when left to itself. Our conscience helps restrain us from acting on our heart's naturally evil desires.

OTHER GUIDES

Some philosophers have proposed a system called "logical positivism" to determine what is right and what is wrong. **Logical positivism** holds that we must, by human experience, test or empirically verify all things to determine if they are right or wrong. The main problem with this is that the statement "we must empirically verify everything to determine if it is right or wrong" is itself not empirically verifiable. It is similar to saying "words have no meaning." Therefore, logical positivism cannot be correct because it is a self-defeating argument.

Still others have proposed that we simply must be ethical people who follow **ethical standards** to determine right and wrong. The problem is that ethics cannot stand alone. One's ethics derive directly from one's view of God and one's personal theology. Ethics must always be based on a foundation. Thus, atheistic ethics have a flimsy foundation and are subject to constant change based on personal whim or public opinion. This approach makes ethics little more than a basic human convention and ultimately it is a form of relativism. One can never say that some action is wrong for all people and at all times. To do this would admit a moral foundation, which is a transcendent foundation that defies explanation in an atheistic worldview.

"Why do we have a conscience?" and "How do we know that our actions are, indeed, correct?" Philosophers such as Aristotle have appealed to a **natural law** that governs humanity's behaviors and gives us a sense of what right is. Problems arise because this law is not concrete nor can all people determine what this law is. That is, there is no universal agreement on the natural law—what it is or prescribes and prohibits. It simply leads to confusion and everyone doing what they think is right. One man cannot judge another's actions; regardless of the outrage it causes the majority. Again, this system, too, leads to a truth that is relative, where contradiction and confusion reign in moral judgments.

Another popular philosophy is the **social contract** put forth primarily by John Locke, who wrote that humanity has a social contract with his fellow man. This contract comprises social norms that enable humanity to evolve into the creatures we are today. The social contract is sort of a gentlemen's agreement that, throughout history, keeps us from killing each other. The main problem with this theory is not all men have a clear vision of this contract. It is simply a social convention that is changeable at any moment by any person in any society and has no solid foundation. In the end, it leads to anarchy.

Aside from leading to relativism, another major problem with the social contract and other schools of secular ethical thought in general is that they rely on *induction*, which, in the realm of the physical world, is always a logical fallacy.

For example, let's say I want to determine the color of crows. As a good scientist, I begin observing crows and recording the results. The first 500 crows I observe are black. If I used induction, I would then generalize that "all crows are black." The problem is that it does not matter whether I observe 500 or 5,000,000 crows, I cannot logically conclude that all crows are black with logical certainty because if only one crow in the world is blue, my statement if false. The only way one I could make this claim was to see every crow in the world. This includes not only every crow alive today, but also every crow that has ever existed. I must look in every place that ever existed to make sure that I did not miss one blue or brown crow perching in a remote part of the earth.

If this were not enough, I must not only look on earth but everywhere in the universe—both at the present moment and for every moment of eternity. Now that is a tall order and, obviously, impossible. Nevertheless, I must do this to ensure there is not one crow hiding out somewhere that is not black in color, which would make my conclusion false.

These theories fail also because they base their conclusions on the logical fallacy of *asserting the consequent*. For example, if I see that the pavement is wet and that it is raining, I might assume that whenever the pavement is wet it is raining. This is asserting the consequent, which is a formal logical fallacy. The wetness of the pavement does not cause the rain, and all wetness on the pavement is not caused by rain. There could be a number of other reasons that the pavement is wet. Maybe a water main broke. Maybe someone hosed it off. Maybe someone spilled water on the street. Maybe it was raining earlier but stopped. There are many factors—besides rain—that could explain why the pavement is wet.

The scientific method is based largely on this fallacy. The scientist conducts experiments and, based on the results, claims that something is true. This is asserting the fallacy of asserting the consequent. The only way we can know truth about the world around us is to have unlimited knowledge and infinite experience beyond our human capabilities that can tell us something we can know is certain. When it comes to non-absolute ventures, such as technology and medicine, science can serve us well without asserting the consequent; science typically looks for cause-and-effect relationships. But science can never answer ultimate questions (such as the origin of the universe, the difference between right and wrong, or whether God exists) because they are beyond empirical verification. They are *not* scientific questions.

The good news is that God has been everywhere, seen everything, and placed the systems we observe and the experiences we have today in their place. Therefore, He is the only One who can say for certain how we are to live. The only true foundation we have is God who has made things clear to us through His revealed Word, the Bible.

Through scripture, God gives us commands to live by and standards to judge both our own actions and the actions of others. He has also provided us a restraint against our own inward desires by instilling in us a conscience that acts as a sort of moral thermostat that tells us when we are about to do wrong. The conscience by no means prevents us from doing wrong, but is a built-in restraint against evil given by His grace. God has not only given us a conscience but also has created and given us **laws of logic**. We can use these to understand the words I write and they allow us to carry on a conversation. Without the laws of logic and systems by which we can live, we can do nothing. God made us in His image, which makes us rational creatures. We have an eternal soul and are able to think and reason, which distinguishes us from animals. This also makes humanity responsible for its own actions. Genesis 9:5-6 says, "And for your lifeblood I will surely demand an accounting. I will demand an accounting from every animal. Moreover, from each man, too, I will demand an accounting for the life of his fellow man. Whoever sheds the blood of man, by man shall his blood be shed; for in the image of God has God made man."

We see a similar statement in the New Testament in Matthew 12:36, "But I tell you that men will have to give account on the Day of Judgment for every careless word they have spoken." We must all give an account before God for the things we have done, whether good or bad, while here on earth. God has not kept silent on what is right and wrong. He has given us His word as our source of truth by which to live. He has given us the Ten Commandments in Exodus 20. He has also inscribed His commands on our hearts by giving us a conscience that convicts us of our wrong deeds. We have been given all we need for determining right and wrong—God's word, the Bible. It is therefore up to us to read it and live by its truths.

CAN MAN LIVE WITHOUT GOD?

Human existence hinges on this question. The statement "There is no God" has much greater impact than the sum of the words, and the impact ripples throughout our culture. It affects the way we treat our fellow man, our ethical standards, our moral conduct, how we approach and understand science, and so on. In short, it impacts our total worldview. Without God, we are simply the outcome of mindless, pointless natural processes with no purpose and no hope for a life beyond this physical existence. We are just a random conglomeration of atoms, the product of a cosmic accident. We serve no purpose and have no lasting effect in a life that is meaningless and worthless. There is no supreme authority to judge right and wrong.

Here is an example of the logical outcome of this premise. Standards vary from culture to culture—what is "true" for one might be "false" for another; what is "good" in one might be "evil" in another. With no God, human life is of no value. Therefore, you cannot say that the life taken for dinner by a band of cannibals was a waste nor can you say that loving your neighbor was good. Both actions, regardless of their outcome, are of equal value and can be morally right. In this worldview, there are no right or wrong—only preferences or cultural *conventions* or *norms*. Some people love their neighbor and some people eat their neighbor. Which do you prefer? Without God, you have no rights. Murder, rape, and sodomy are not wrong but perfectly natural expressions of our desires. I think this concept is best illustrated by this poem.

Paul Elwell

CREED

by Steve Turner

This is the creed I have written on behalf of all of us.
We believe in Marx, Freud, and Darwin
We believe everything is OK
as long as you don't hurt anyone,
to the best of your definition of hurt,
and to the best of your knowledge.

> Steve Turner illustrates the bankrupt beliefs of those who put their faith in men, who lack a sufficient foundation for providing a comprehensive belief system for humanity.

We believe in sex before, during, and after marriage.
We believe in the therapy of sin.
We believe that adultery is fun.
We believe that sodomy is OK.
We believe that taboos are taboo.

> The pursuit of pleasure and sin are acceptable in this type of society, which places a higher value on a lack of limitations and the "virtue" of tolerance more than anything else.

We believe that everything is getting better
despite evidence to the contrary.
The evidence must be investigated
And you can prove anything with evidence.

> This illustrates the humanistic point of view that humanity is getting better. This is what many political theories rely upon. They believe that humans are basically good despite evidence of evil in the world, such as what was perpetrated by Hitler, Stalin and Mussolini.

We believe there's something in
horoscopes, UFOs and bent spoons;
Jesus was a good man
just like Buddha, Mohammed, and ourselves.

He was a good moral teacher
although we think His good morals were bad.
We believe that all religions are basically the same--
at least the one that we read was.
They all believe in love and goodness.
They only differ on matters of
creation, sin, heaven, hell, God, and salvation.

The push toward Unitarianism is constant in culture as people want to be able to say everyone is right and never have to offend anyone. The problem is that not everyone can be right as illustrated in the chapter on absolute truth.

We believe that after death comes the Nothing
Because when you ask the dead what happens, they say nothing.
If death is not the end, if the dead have lied,
then it's compulsory heaven for all
excepting perhaps Hitler, Stalin, and Genghis Khan.

The two extremes of religion that attempt to appeal to the masses are the Unitarian view of the universal heaven and the atheistic view that life ends at death. There is only way we could know what happens after death. That is if someone has been there and was able to tell us.

We believe in Masters and Johnson.
What's selected is average.
What's average is normal.
What's normal is good.

The majority determining what is right is a dangerous combination as the majority can be wrong. Just because it is popular does not mean it is right. It was popular to have slaves in the American south but it was not right.

We believe in total disarmament.
We believe there are direct links between warfare and bloodshed.
Americans should beat their guns into tractors
and the Russians would be sure to follow.
We believe that man is essentially good.

It's only his behavior that lets him down.
This is the fault of society.
Society is the fault of conditions.
Conditions are the fault of society.

> This illustrates the idealistic state of the humanist who believes that we are evolving into something better than what we are currently. They reject all the evidence around them that shows mankind is getting worse, not better, because it would disprove their core belief.

We believe that each man must find the truth that is right for him.
Reality will adapt accordingly.
The universe will readjust.
History will alter.
We believe that there is no absolute truth
excepting the truth that there is no absolute truth.

> This non-sense is illustrated in that the rejection of absolute truth is foolish and leads to an unsustainable worldview. Those who do accept this rejection of truth cannot live consistent with the worldview they claim.

We believe in the rejection of creeds,
and the flowering of individual thought.
If chance be the Father of all flesh,
disaster is his rainbow in the sky,
and when you hear:
State of Emergency!
Sniper Kills Ten!
Troops on Rampage!
Whites go Looting!
Bomb Blasts School!
It is but the sound of man worshiping his maker. (Zacharias, 1994)

Though the poem is an ode to simple-minded thinking, it does illustrate the consequence of rejecting God who is necessary for life. The use of logic, science, and objective, moral, or ethical standards are established on the basis of the existence of a transcendent, unchanging

God who provides these standards. As we discussed in the previous chapter on absolute truth, there is an objective, absolute standard of truth by which we can judge truth from falsehood. The atheist argument fails, in fact, because it relies on the Christian worldview. It borrows a firm objective foundation on which to base its moral judgments. Its foundations must be based on something higher than mere human preference, which the atheist worldview is not. The debate is not over facts and laws that govern the universe we live in but the final reference point by which we understand all facts and laws.

For example, I can look at the Grand Canyon and say, "It is amazing what the Genesis flood created in just a very short period of time." Meanwhile the atheist looks at it and says, "Look at what millions even billions of years of ocean sediment have laid down." We look at the same facts, the Grand Canyon, but our points of reference are different. I look at it through the unchanging word of God, the Bible, by seeing God to be logical, unchanging, and good. His character is evident in the world around us. This renders logic, science, ethics, and every other element of human experience meaningless apart from the belief in the God of the Bible. The atheist looks at the Grand Canyon through the constantly changing theory of evolution.

My point here is not to argue the theory of evolution and its various flaws, but to show how two reasonable people looking at the same facts can disagree on what brought them about. The point is that both theist and atheist have foundational views. God's view is unchanging, and His character is the basis for judging right and wrong. He gave us rules and laws of logic, mathematics, moral standards, and a transcendent ethic to live by. When evaluating any other worldview or system of thought, we must ask the defining question: Does this standard for human behavior come from one who is above us and who can give a common point of reference or ethic for all humanity? If this standard does not—meaning that it comes merely from a finite perspective of another human being—then its worldview, carried to its logical conclusions, will lead to arbitrariness, absurdity, or inconsistency. To form a coherent worldview, we must base our understanding of human experience on the permanent and unchanging principles. The atheistic worldview must base itself on God's permanent and unchanging standards to understand the world around us.

Without God, life consists only of matter and motion. Objects are amoral: neither good *nor* bad. There is no standard by which to judge them. For example, is a hammer a right or a wrong object? I think most people would agree it is neither; it is amoral. Let's say someone brutally crushes a child's skull with that hammer. Is that hammer good or bad? The answer is unchanged: the hammer itself is neither right nor wrong. We can use it to perform an act that is good or evil, within the Christian framework, right or wrong, but the hammer itself remains neither.

If we are just material whose existence ends with our last breath, how can we say that savage murder is wrong in any objective sense of the word? For if matter is all that exists then nothing is moral. Even humans are amoral because they are, like the hammer, just objects composed of so many atoms and molecules. The central problem with the atheist worldview is that it relies on arbitrary standards for understanding human experience, most of which are formed from prejudice, comfort, or social pressure. For example, prejudice may influence one's belief system because of a pre-commitment to materialism. Materialism states that matter is all that has ever existed, and to admit a supernatural, super-material realm would defeat the materialist system of thought. Hence, the idea of supernatural existence is ruled out without consideration. With no absolute moral standard to tell them, what they are doing is wrong, what's to stop them from doing whatever they please? Nothing. This is comfortable; it does not require any behavior modification—anything goes.

Social pressure can also influence one's system of thought. Society—and western society in particular—has largely accepted this materialistic view of the universe, and people who believe otherwise are often dismissed as unscientific or naïve. Those influenced by social pressure give in to what the majority believes. Even most ethical atheists, however, believe in standards of human conduct lest anarchy prevail! This provides common ground because, though we disagree on what the ultimate standard for the standards of conduct, we agree that "murder" and "theft" are not socially desirable. The question boils down to: Who sets this standard of moral conduct by which we are to live our lives?

The Christian's answer is perfectly logical: God is the only source for objective truth, the laws of logic, and physical laws because we observe all of these in the universe He created. They are absolute, unchanging, and without beginning, since God Himself is eternal. Since we humans were made in the image of God, we are capable of understanding and using these laws. Without these solid, absolute foundations, society would be consumed in chaos, but God gives us a solid meaning and moral foundation on which to base our lives. Dennis Prager, during a debate with an atheist, said, "If you were in a dark alley in South Central Los Angeles and saw 10 young men walking toward you, would you be more at ease if you knew the men had just come from a Bible study?" (Prager, 1992) This is a humorous quip, but it serves to illustrate that the Bible does give us a standard of right and wrong and encourages us to love our neighbor. This standard is not arbitrary but fixed for humankind to live by for all time. God gave us these foundations in His word, the Bible. He shows us the way to live and the proper way to treat our fellow man, and He provides a way of freedom from our sinful desires. Left to our own devices, without the change of heart that only God can bring, our sinful nature leads us to follow our evil desires.

We see this godless evil in the notable 20th century atheist dictators Mussolini, Stalin, and Mao. Their brutal reigns of terror resulted in killing millions of people in the pursuit of godless regimes. Psalm 10:4 says, "The wicked in his proud countenance does not seek God; God is in none of his thoughts." We see that man, left to himself, does not seek God but only his own self-interest. We must understand our underlying problem. We are by nature self-centered, seeking fulfillment of our own desires. This was the result of our rebellion against God and His standards (Genesis 3). There is hope, however: "This is love: not that we loved God, but that He loved us and sent his Son as an atoning sacrifice for our sins" (1 John 4:10).

In His love for us, God sought after us and gave us a way to come back to Him, regardless of our wanderings and sinful rebellion. We must, however, accept His gift of salvation. The cure for the heart seeking everything but God and His truth is a relationship with Jesus Christ. God will give us a new heart with a new desire that seeks Him and wants to please Him.

DON'T ALL RELIGIONS
LEAD TO GOD?

The simple and logical answer is no. The laws of logic give us a simple concept to follow when comparing different religions. The Law of Non-Contradiction states that a fact is either this or that, not *both* this and that simultaneously. It is common in the eastern part of the world to use a different type of logic called the "both/and" system of logic. This logical position states that it is not one thing or another but both things and each other. Though this might make for a nice mind game, it is not practiced in real-life situations. Ravi Zacharias illustrates that though in his homeland of India they say they believe in the both/and system of logic, they still look both ways prior to crossing the street. (Zacharias, 2000) This is because they know in real life that a space can only be occupied by the bus or you, not both you and the bus at the same time.

This is quite foundational in nature because most religions—not just Christianity–make some claim of exclusivity. Islam claims that Allah is God and no other, and Jews believe Yahweh is God and no other. The logical problem is that not all of these positions can be true. It is either one or the other. They cannot all be correct. They cannot all be true because it violates the Law of Non-Contradiction. If mutually contradicting statements can both be true, all is nonsense.

The main objection to the position that "there is only one way to God" is that it excludes all others and says they are wrong. Many people dismiss this as "exclusionary and arrogant." They find it hard to believe that people who sincerely believe in a religion—*any* religion—could be sent to hell. The problem with the argument "it doesn't matter what you believe as long as you are sincere" is that it is possible, in a world of absolute truth, to be sincerely wrong. For example, someone can sincerely believe that hitting someone in the head with a two-by-four will not hurt that person. The laws of physics, however, do not change based on that person's misconception; no matter how sincerely he believes it. The truth, of course, is that being hit in the head with a two-by-four can result in serious injury or death, no matter whether the one striking or the one struck believes it.

This is even upheld by our court system. Take a man accused of murder whose defense is that he did not agree with laws against murder. This defense is hardly persuasive and will not likely result in a not-guilty verdict. The law is independent of his beliefs in it. Now someone could say it is "arrogant" for the court to impose its value system on this man who does not believe in it. The result would be anarchy and chaos.

How a religion or your perception of God makes you feel does not matter. We cannot judge truth or the existence of God based on how the conclusion makes us feel. Truth is independent of our feelings and exists whether we like it or not. What really matters is the truth, no matter how sincere our belief to the contrary may be. The "enlightened" answer to this is expressed commonly in Reverend Loveshade's parable of the elephant and the five blind men.

One day, five blind men, who knew nothing of elephants, went to examine one to find out what it was. Reaching out randomly each touched it in a different spot. One man touched the side, one an ear, one a leg, one a tusk, and one the trunk. Each satisfied that he now knew the true nature of the beast; they all sat down to discuss it.

> *"We now know that the elephant is like a wall," said the one who touched the side. "The evidence is conclusive."*
>
> *"I believe you are mistaken, sir," said the one who touched an ear. "The elephant is more like a large fan."*
>
> *"You are both wrong," said the leg man. "The creature is obviously like a tree."*
>
> *"A tree?" questioned the tusk toucher. "How can you mistake a spear for a tree?"*

> *"What?" said the trunk feeler, "a spear is long and round, but anyone knows it doesn't move. Couldn't you feel the muscles? It is definitely a type of snake! A blind man could see that!" said the fifth blind man. (Loveshade, 2010).*

The person who tells this story normally goes on to conclude that everyone is partly right in their view of God; we all see a part of God but not the whole thing. Therefore, no one has the whole picture of God. The problem is that the story assumes the person telling the story has a complete unbiased picture of God. They conclude that just as the blind men could not fully see the elephant, so we religious people cannot fully see God and thus we should accept all religions as equally valid since they are all "partly" correct. The problem is, these blind men are not equally correct in their assertions that the elephant is a wall, a fan, a tree, a snake, and a spear; in fact, they are all equally wrong. No part of the elephant is any of those things!

This story is a better illustration that all religions are equally wrong than that they are equally true. The intent of the story is to illustrate that there is a higher view that does not exclude any other views. Since we know, logically, that absolute truth exists we know that this is false because no view that includes all views can exist. For instance, even the most inclusive person will most likely exclude Hitler's or Stalin's view of God from a list of views. In a world where absolute truth exists, it is nonsense to claim that everyone's view is true. It is a clear contradiction because truth, by definition, is mutually exclusive and cannot be unique to every person. The Law of Non-Contradiction shows it is not possible for all religions to be true because they all make mutually exclusive claims. In fact, based on the Law of Non-Contradiction, it is more likely that all religions are false than that they are all true. Truth is exclusive, and there is only one truth as the law states. As Steve Turner stated in his poem **Creed:**

> "Jesus was a good man just like Buddha, Mohammed and ourselves. We believe he was a good teacher of morals but we believe that his good morals are really bad. We believe that all religions are basically the same, at least the one we read was,

they all believe in love and goodness, they only differ on matters of creation, sin, heaven, hell, God and salvation."

C.S Lewis put it quite clearly in his book **Mere Christianity**:

"I am trying here to prevent anyone saying the really foolish thing that people often say about Him: 'I'm ready to accept Jesus as a great moral teacher, but I don't accept His claim to be God.' That is the one thing we must not say. A man who was merely a man and said the sort of things Jesus said would not be a great moral teacher. He would either be a lunatic – on a level with the man who says he is a poached egg – or else he would be the Devil of Hell. You must make your choice. Either this man was, and is, the Son of God, or else a madman or something worse. You can shut him up for a fool, you can spit at Him and kill Him as a demon; or you can fall at His feet and call him Lord and God. But let us not come with any patronizing nonsense about his being a great human teacher. He has not left that open to us. He did not intend to." (Lewis, 1952)"

The religions of the world are mutually exclusive. Some, such as Islam and Judaism, acknowledge the existence of Jesus (albeit as less than God's Son and the Savior of the world), but they cannot all be correct. The main difference between these religions and the truth is: Christianity is the only "religion" that came from God to man. It is not the type of religion man would make up. By contrast, the other world religions—Islam, Buddhism, Hinduism, Judaism—are from man to God. They strive to make us humans feel better about our universal problem of sin, shame, and our inability to do good when left to our own efforts. What I mean by this is that religions that are from man to God (i.e., all religions other than Christianity) share a theme expressed in different ways: They try to earn man's way out of guilt by good works, good deeds, giving to the poor, and other religious acts and rituals.

The problems of sin and guilt are universal, meaning we are all born with them. By sin and guilt I mean that we know what we ought to do but do not do it because all humanity is born with a sinful nature. We have a law written on our hearts, which we can suppress, but it is there naturally. Works-based deeds are the most appealing way of getting rid of this feeling of guilt and shame. This is the attraction of some religions. Because I do good things "A, B and C" I know I am okay with God and can live my life otherwise as I please. Doing good things or comparing ourselves to others who aren't as good helps us feel better. In Islam, one can say: "I'm sure my good deeds outweigh my bad, so I am okay with God." In Judaism, one can say: "I participate in Yom Kippur, the Day of Atonement, so I am okay with God for the next year." This is like taking a drug for pain while your hand is resting flat on the burner of a hot stove. It may take care of the pain temporarily—the symptom, but it ignores the real source of the problem: Your hand is still on the hot stove. We search for a remedy that removes the source of the guilt and shame. This is how humanity deals with the problem of sin and shame.

Christianity, however, has something that no other world religion has—grace. Grace is the defining factor in a religion that originates with God rather than with man. God does everything and man does nothing. God sent His Son, Jesus, to come and bridge the separation between us and God that was caused by our sin. Only a sinless man born without a sinful nature could pay the penalty for the sins of all humanity. It couldn't be one of us because we were all born with this nature. Jesus is that man. He came and died in our place. He made a way for us to be forgiven of all our sin and have our guilt taken away. In fact, Jesus did more than just pay the penalty of our sins; He conquered death in the process through His resurrection from the dead. Acts 4:12 says, "There is salvation in no one else; for there is no other name under heaven that has been given among men, by which we must be saved." The author of Acts, Luke was referring, of course, to the name of Jesus Christ. The substitution of Christ's death (in our place) enables us to be at peace with God. We must accept His gift of salvation. Outside of the sacrificial death and resurrection of Christ, there is no other hope for mankind.

Is there a God?

We are all rational creatures. This fact in and of itself is evidence for the existence of God. The logical processes and orderly systems in which we live suggest that there must be some objective standard by which we can measure and judge things. All human observation in the scientific disciplines and all studies of the world around us are only based on the assumption that the world is an orderly place that operates according to laws and principles that can be studied and discovered. If there were no order and we could not subject the observations around us to logical examination, there would be no point to mathematics, the sciences, philosophy, or linguistics because it is not possible to make sense of chaos. Science and all human knowledge presuppose a systematic, orderly world.

So the world must originate from a higher standard than the human mind. No human mind can create universal standards by which we can measure and examine the world around us. The logical problem is induction. We humans simply cannot make absolute statements about the world on the basis of induction. As we discussed earlier, inductive statements about nature cannot be logically true without God. The solution to the dilemma of induction is that only God can make inductive statements because only He has been everywhere and seen everything for all time. Therefore, when God gives us true, inductive statements (as only He can) in the Bible, we understand them to be words we can live by. The Bible with its inductive statements from God Himself is the only source of real truth upon which we can base our lives.

Scientific knowledge is based on the scientific method, which is a probable method of discovery and the best available to us. True, logical, defensible scientific discovery requires the scientist to use a method that does not commit the fallacy of asserting the consequent. Let's examine the fallacy of asserting the consequent once again. A typical example of this formal logical fallacy is:

1.   When it rains, the streets are wet.
2.   Therefore, if the streets are wet, it must be raining.

The problem, of course, is that the street could be wet for any number of other reasons. A sprinkler could have sprayed water on the street. Or perhaps it rained earlier and the streets have not dried off yet (even though it is not raining now). This fallacy is what science uses to determine truth. Thus science cannot be used as a method to determine what is true in any ultimate sense; it can only report the results of experiments on phenomena that can be measured empirically (i.e., by the senses: taste, touch, smell, sight, and hearing).

Thus, when it comes to accounting for a phenomenon such as conscience, science is at a loss to explain it. Its existence is not explainable by normal human means. The basis for science is coherent only if there is a God who provides an unchanging standard by which we can expect experiments to produce the same results today, as they will 10 years or 100 years from now. This unchanging standard is the basis science must assume to gain a foundation for knowledge. Imagine a world in which gravity worked today but did not work two weeks from now. God gives us a foundation that we can use to conduct experimentation and gain understanding of the world around us through science.

Science, however, is at a loss to account for phenomena that cannot be explored empirically. Take conscience as an example. Conscience is a gift from God that defies empirical investigation. It serves as a guide to what we should do and should not do. Because of this gift of conscience we must one day give an account for what we have done—both right and wrong. According to the Law, if we have committed even one wrong deed in our lives, we will be condemned to hell. Conversely, God has provided a way for us to be acceptable to Him. Our sin has offended the holy God, who cannot allow sin to go unpunished. But He sent

Jesus, His son, to come to earth and live a morally perfect life. Thus, Jesus was the only One who did not deserve punishment for sin.

To redeem us, God placed all of our sins upon Jesus, who bore the punishment for our sins. Jesus suffered the eternal punishment each of us deserved while on the cross. Therefore, when God looks at us, He no longer sees our sins (because, as the apostle Paul states, we are "hidden in Christ with God") because our debt was paid in full at the cross. For our part, all we must do is simply accept the gift of salvation Jesus offers.

Psalm 15:1 says, "The fool says in his heart, 'There is no God.'" We must understand that the person who holds the view "there is no God" is not being intellectually honest with himself. He is making this statement out of ignorance since, as we saw above, he cannot know everything and has not observed everything for all time. Many atheists are intelligent and educated, but they reject the only source of truth, the word of God.

What is the Meaning of Life?

Since the dawn of human history, people have sought to find meaning and purpose in life. We will examine three of the more popular answers to the question "What is the meaning of life?" Four main pursuits people seek meaning in are: (1) wealth and material possessions, (2) worldly pleasures, (3) accomplishments, and (4) relationships.

Wealth

Many people try to find meaning in wealth. We are not just thinking of the super-rich or millionaires in our culture either but also about those who work overtime to buy that new toy—a new car, a big-screen TV, a video game, etc. They are among those who horde money for retirement, more than they could ever spend, seeking to find meaning in wealth. Some work hard to buy things they do not need simply to impress people they do not really like. I think John D. Rockefeller most dramatically expresses this obsession. When a young reporter asked the billionaire how many millions it took to satisfy a man, Rockefeller responded, "The next million." Another super-rich man, Andrew Carnegie, who made a fortune in steel, when asked "How much is enough?" responded: "Just a little more." (Carnegie, 1913-1918)

How many times have we heard of wealthy doctors, lawyers, politicians, and multi-millionaires who, after devoting their lives to building massive empires, end up committing suicide? Their problem with accumulating massive wealth was that they believed that wealth would make them happy or satisfy their deepest longings or solve all their problems. That is a lie, but unfortunately, there is no end to this cycle. You can always accumulate more and more money, and having it all is a goal beyond reaching (even for the likes Rockefeller and Carnegie). Inevitably, the day will come when the wealth-chasers will stop (because of old age, ill health, or utter exhaustion) and look back at their work and find it is an empty hole. The promise of meaning, joy, and fulfillment in wealth is a lie that we sometimes confuse with the American way. It is a lie nonetheless, for wealth and the prestige it brings can never satisfy our longings and pursuing it at the expense of all else will only leave us in ruins and/or alone. Once you reach this level, the saddest realization is that it leads to emptiness.

WORLDLY PLEASURES

Others try to fulfill their longing for meaning and purpose through pleasurable pursuits. Some seek pleasure in various sexual activities; some indulge in drinking to the point of intoxication or the so-called "recreational" use of drugs (prescription or illegal) as a way to mask the pain of an empty life. Few would deny that life is not challenging at times, but these pleasures are not the solution but tend merely to cover up the real pain people face inside. Instead of facing the reality of our need for true meaning and purpose, people try to drown their pain with alcohol or kill the pain with drugs. These simply postpone the inevitable reality that we all must face.

Another form of worldly pleasure seeking as a means of finding fulfillment is entertainment. These people are sensation-seekers, "party animals" who love to socialize and usually dislike being alone for any length of time. They "vacation hard" to find value in the memories they build while having fun. These folks are easily bored and want to move to the next exciting thing in their lives. Many times, they speed through the early portion of their lives looking forward to the next fun activity and spend the latter part of their lives looking back at the fun they had. Regardless, they are never fully satisfied.

ACCOMPLISHMENTS

Still others try to find meaning in accomplishments. They strive to do all the hard and impressive things this world values. They work hard to impress others and find their value in the way others respond to their successes and achievements. For some, it might be one more academic degree or one more promotion that leads them to the next rung on the corporate ladder. For others, it is a hole-in-one when golfing or an award ceremony or recognition for doing something extraordinary. Often such people find themselves depressed when they show someone all they have worked for only to find that the other person is unimpressed (or not impressed *enough*).

RELATIONSHIPS

Yet others strive to find meaning in relationships. These people are like the girl on a college or high school campus who must always have a boyfriend because she finds meaning only when she is in a relationship. She goes from one empty relationship to the next telling herself the same lie: "The next one will give me the love, meaning, and purpose I've been longing for." This is a self-destructive cycle and she often finds that each new relationship is worse than the last.

Then there are those married men or women who find no purpose or fulfillment in their own spouse and start looking for someone else to fill the void. They leave behind their current life, spouse, and children to pursue momentary pleasures and passionate relationships. Unfortunately, such relationships bring only temporary meaning (if any) and only leave them increasingly empty with each passing day.

All of these attempts to fill our deepest longings and struggles to find meaning in life are like Vicodin (a painkiller) for the soul. They offer a little ease from the pain, but in the end it always comes back. The real pain is deep in our soul and we long to find the cure. We take the temporary painkillers of wealth, pleasure, accomplishments, and relationships to give us momentary relief. In the end the pain returns and makes us yearn for something more substantial, not just to kill the painful symptom but also to cure the disease causing the pain.

THE REAL MEANING

When considering the question of the meaning of life, one of the first things we must ask is: Why do we need meaning? Meaning brings purpose, a reason to get up in the morning, something to keep us from committing suicide to escape the dark and difficult seasons of life. Meaning gives us a reason to care about others and something to live for beyond our own selfish desires. To establish meaning, we must first look at how we got where we are. If we have no source of origin—no creator—and the universe is eternal with no beginning, we truly have no purpose, for we can make no lasting impact in this world. "All we are," as the doleful Kansas song says, "is dust in the wind." (Kansas, 1978) We are here today and blown away tomorrow, and all that's left is a fleeting memory before we are forever forgotten. The things we do or do not do here do not matter. All that matters is doing things that give us temporary pleasure or feelings of satisfaction, but in the end, they are meaningless.

A life devoid of value and worth flows logically from an evolutionary worldview. Why are we here? We are the product of a non-intelligent natural process. This means our life is ultimately purposeless. We are nothing more than the highest animal, no different from lower life forms or even non-living objects. We have no value above that we ascribe to a cow or a pig. We are just purposeless beings who are born, live, and then die. We have no source for moral judgments since there is no supreme law that everyone agrees to live by. Our hearts are empty and longing for meaning and purpose...but we are destined to find none.

The cure for a life of purposelessness is best illustrated by St. Augustine who said: "You have created us for Yourself, and our hearts are restless till they find their rest in You." (Hippo, AD 397-398) We find our meaning in the worship, the reverence, and the faith we have in the promises of God. God, our Creator, is the source of truth and He has given us our life's purpose. Since He created us, He made us for a specific purpose. Mankind receives value as His creation because we are made in the image of God, according to Genesis 1:26-27. God has given us the gift of rationality, placing us above the rest of creation. This unique gift from God, who created us, can only be fully understood in the context of a relationship with Him. This is the only thing that will satisfy the soul. Another aspect of being created in the image of God is that we humans have received the gift of being able to enjoy beauty. Have you ever walked in the woods and thought it looked like a painting?

God has created us in His image, unique above all creation, for Himself. God fills the needs of the human heart by giving us an objective source of truth in His revelation to mankind expressed in the Bible. He has given us an object worthy of our worship—Himself. G.K.

Chesterton said, "God is like the sun; you cannot look at it, but without it, you cannot look at anything else." (Lewis, 1952)

He has given all people the ability to see and understand life around us. Many things that are good in this world lead to meaninglessness without God. Once we see these good things in the light of God, however, we find meaning and purpose that enable us to truly enjoy these good things. God has given us hope for the future. If we place our trust in Him, we will be together with Him forever. He has shown us the wonder of His power in creation, the awe of His grace, and the amazement of His goodness to humanity. Fulfilling meaning must come from something that is larger than us.

Our pursuit of the things that give life meaning ends successfully only with a relationship with Jesus Christ. He is the only way to God. So what is the meaning of life? Why are we here? The Westminster Confession of Faith states it best: "It is our purpose in life to worship God and to enjoy him forever." (Faith, n.d.)

How do I know that I know?

The question "How do I know that I know?" (also known as epistemology—the study of knowledge) is often overlooked or not considered by most people. So why is it important? Epistemology is the theory of knowledge of how we are convinced that something is true. More simply stated it is "how we know that we know."

We all claim to have information about something. Take gravity, for example. We all claim to know about gravity, but how do we know that this information is correct? Is it just because we have been taught that there is a law of gravity? Is it that we have experienced objects falling to the ground so many times that we believe it is true for all people and for all time? Is it because we observe that what goes up must come down?

What if, for one period of time in history, things were different from what we experience today? Suppose, instead of falling to the ground, objects stayed still in the air and levitated? If there were a single case in history when an object with mass stayed in the air, our knowledge about gravity would be incorrect.

Consider the naturalistic view of epistemology. Materialism assumes there is nothing more than what we see and observe here in our universe. Space, time, energy, and motion are all that exist. They depend on human rationality as their source of information. They might answer the question "I know that I know" because I can reason it out logically, or because, through rational experimentation, I can test and measure a result. This epistemology depends on our senses and mind to be our source of truth. Therefore, the mind and its ability to reason give us our source of knowledge.

The Christian view of epistemology begins similarly because we use reason, experiments, and human experience to determine some truth. This is not, however, the foundation for truth but rather a by-product of the way we discover truth. We receive truth and our foundation for reasoning from a source of infinite knowledge—from God—in two ways. First, we receive God's infinite knowledge using our rationality to examine the world around us and apply the laws of logic to our findings. These laws are unchanging, infinite, and true for all time and in all situations because they are given by an unchanging God. God's sustaining hand is what makes scientific experimentation possible. God promised Noah in Genesis 8:22:

> *"As long as the earth endures, seedtime and harvest, cold and heat, summer and winter, day and night will never cease."*

This promise is what allows us to expect that the results of experiments we conduct today will continue to occur the same way in the future. God's sustaining hand holds all natural laws in place and because of this we can explore the world and make new discoveries about it. This is the basis for all science and discovery and the scientific method relies upon it. This allows us to know that what we discover will not change the next time we examine it in the future.

Second, we alone among all the creatures in creation have been given this source of true knowledge because we are made in the image of God and are able to think His thoughts after Him, which is the basis of logic. The naturalist worldview cannot account for the laws of logic. They must consider them to be a social convention that man has come up with or just use them pragmatically because they seem to work on everything of which we apply them.

The problem is that in order to deny the laws of logic one must use the laws of logic to disprove them. For example, if I say that the Law of Non-Contradiction is untrue, I am saying that it is not true and something else is. This implies both cannot be true; it must be one or the other. Therefore, to disprove the Law of Non-Contradiction, I had to use the law that proves it is true, while trying to disprove it. God gave us logic to examine and make sense of this world, and our examination depends on Him and what He has revealed.

The Bible, God's word, is the source of all truth. God, who is infinite in knowledge and omnipresent in all of history and time, has revealed this source of truth by which we can form our theory of knowledge. Though the Bible is not a science textbook it provides a foundation for knowledge that we can build upon. God have given us a solid foundation that allows us to study the world around us in meaningful ways. For example, we can base our knowledge of mathematics on the Bible. God showed us, through His Word, mathematical examples that allow us to know that $1 + 1 = 2$ and not 4. For example, Genesis 5:3-5 states that when Adam had lived 130 years, he had a son in his own likeness, in his own image, and he named him Seth. After Seth was born, Adam lived 800 years and had other sons and daughters. Altogether, Adam lived 930 years, and then he died.

Adam lived $800 + 130 = 930$

The Bible, which is direct revelation from God, shows us that mathematics is not just some random theory that happens to work. We use it because it is true for all people for all time. Along with addition God's word reveals the principles of multiplication, division, counting, subtraction, etc.

So in considering the theory of knowledge, how do we know murder is wrong? An intellectually honest atheist would contend that murder is wrong because it threatens the survival of the race. The Christian will say murder is wrong because God, who possesses infinite knowledge, says it is wrong within His written instruction for humanity. It is a reliable point of reference. For example, almost everyone at one time or another has been sitting in a car, either parked or at an intersection, when the car next to you starts to move. For a moment it feels as though you are moving backward when in fact the other car is moving forward. What do you do? Most people look for a tree, a light post, or some other stationary object to determine whether they are moving backward or if the other car is moving forward. Why do we do this? Because we know that a tree does not move. Therefore, it can be a reference point to reveal whether we are moving or not.

In the same way, the Bible is our reference point in life. God and His standard, revealed in the Bible, is our point of reference that never moves. It is fully reliable to use as our reference point in life. The system of logic God has given us in His written revelation has provided us a perfectly consistent foundation for understanding the world around us. It enables us to know that we know with certainty.

How did I get here?

The question of what happens to us once we die starts with the questions: "Why am I here?" "How did I get here?" and "Do I have any worth apart from the metal traces and basic elements making up this human body I live in?" The most common theory proposed to answer the question "How did we get here?" is evolution. This theory is used to explain the origins of the universe and life on earth without reference to God or theistic influence. The primary problem with evolution is that it is not science but religion. Evolutionary theory is used to explain and justify an atheistic worldview; they are interdependent. The reason the theory of evolution is a religion and not science is that its proponents must take by faith what they were not present to explain and cannot subject to empirical verification (i.e., the scientific method). Events in the distant past are not scientifically verifiable and must be taken by faith.

Science is defined as "knowledge covering general truths of the operation of general laws, as obtained and tested through scientific method and concerned with the physical world" (Dictionary, n.d.). True science is testable, observable, measurable, and repeatable. For example, the law of gravity is testable. To test it all you have to do is drop an object and observe gravity as the object falls down to the ground, not up to the sky. It is repeatable in that the results can be duplicated multiple times with the same measurements from physics.

By definition, therefore, evolution cannot be science. Evolution is not testable, as its processes are said to take millions of years. No one has lived long enough to observe everything that evolutionary faith tells us took place. Who can test the theory? Evolution is also not observable because the human race has never observed it occurring on a macro scale (such as a species evolving to another species). Thus, it takes a lot of faith to believe that an immeasurable, untestable, unobservable "science" could involve processes that are observed nowhere in the realm of science that we can measure, test, and observe. Those who believe in evolution depend on the god of time to make up for all the missing pieces their theory does cannot account for.

Science does not make value judgments, but simply records, tests, and gathers facts. For example, science cannot determine which life is more valuable—a polar bear or a human being. It can simply observe that, when threatened, the polar will maul or kill the human or the human will shoot and kill the polar bear. The scientist who goes beyond the constraints of science and the scientific method reveals his presuppositions. Presuppositions are the core beliefs we hold to and through which filter our experiences. (Someone has said that presuppositions are a matter of "believing is seeing," meaning that we interpret events and experiences based on our core beliefs.) We all have presuppositions that influence how we interpret the world around us. The presuppositions that evolutionary "scientists" hold include:

1. God does not exist.
2. Material is all that exists and it is absolute.
3. The supernatural cannot exist.
4. Our senses are capable of correctly observing and interpreting the entire universe.

It is clear that these presuppositions are biased by a pre-commitment to materialism. This means their worldview only allows for explanations that occur within nature, and nothing outside of this is possible. Therefore, all their conclusions stem from this pre-commitment. The belief is a supernatural explanation cannot exist to anything that occurs in nature. The presupposition is that there is nothing "supernatural." Therefore, the possibility of a supernatural explanation is ruled out as "impossible" prior to examination.

On top of this, they also presuppose that, from our position within the universe, we can correctly observe and test the world and universe around us. This is really an article of faith since we cannot see all things happening now, much less all things that have happened at all times. For example when you look at a set of train tracks they are parallel lines. The distance between them will be the same at your current location as it is 10 miles ahead of you. If you look down the tracks, however, you notice that they meet at a point in the distance. This is called seeing something in perspective. From this vantage point, these tracks appear to meet in the distance (as the sky and earth meet on the horizon), but in reality, they do not: The tracks remain equidistant and parallel.

Similarly, because we are within the universe, we do not have the correct vantage point to determine, without error, if what we see and observe is true or if it is just a matter of our perspective. The only accurate perspective and the only view that can be held with true certainty is one that has seen all things at all times and everywhere for all of eternity. While inside of an object, we see things from our limited perspective. To have a fuller understanding of what we are observing, we must have a full view of the object over the course of its entire history.

Partial knowledge inhibits our understanding; we can only understand things as we see from our limited perspective and not as they actually are. We all depend on our presuppositions. All of us have regressions of beliefs—a series of beliefs that lead us to a final foundational principle. For example, if I believe killing other people is wrong, my regression might go like this.

1. Killing is wrong because it hurts people.
2. Hurting people is wrong because it makes them feel bad.
3. Making people feel bad is not following the golden rule, which is "Do unto others as you would have others do unto you."
4. The golden rule is right because it is in the Bible.
5. The Bible is right because it is the word of God.
6. God's words are the final authority on life and conduct.

We all end up with some final standard on which we base all other judgments. We all believe a certain way about each thing we come across in life, depending on how it fits within our underlying belief system. Because of this we take our foundation, or presuppositions, as fact and rarely challenge them. If we accept the scientific worldview of materialism, as evolutionists do, we lose purpose in life. In his article "Evolution as Religion," David Unfred presented the following consequences of accepting scientific or materialistic presuppositions:

> *"Thus there was no historic Adam and Eve who were sinless creatures created in the image of God. There was no historic Fall of mankind because of original sin. Death was not a penalty of sin, since death has always been an inseparable part of life from the beginning. And what of the atoning work of Christ on the cross? His death is not needed because the process marches onward and upward. So would argue the evolutionist." (Unfred, March 1982)*

When we accept these concepts we lose meaning in life. We no longer have an explanation for evil. We lose the concept of a moral law and its implication for such moral reasoning as to why we should not murder. We no longer have respect for unborn human life. We lose the capacity to say euthanasia is objectively and inherently wrong. We have no need to atone for our sinful deeds because there is no sin and thus no standard by which to declare actions evil. Rather, the most we can say is that certain actions are against someone's ideas of what life should look like. This is the underlying problem with evolutionary/atheistic presuppositions: It lacks the capacity to infuse life with meaning and morality. The logical problem with this worldview is that not everyone's presuppositions are true; they cannot all be true. Ken Ham illustrates this in his book *The Lie*. He records a conversation with a geology professor:

> *I once debated with a geology professor from an American university on a radio program. He said that evolution was real science because evolutionists were prepared to continually change their theories as they found new data. He said that creation was not science because a creationist's views were set by the Bible and, therefore, were not subject to change.*
>
> *I answered, "The reason scientific theories change is because we don't know everything, isn't it? We don't have all the evidence."*
>
> *"Yes, that's right," he said.*
>
> *I replied, "But, we will never know everything."*
>
> *"That's true," he answered.*
>
> *I then stated, "We will always continue to find new evidence."*

> *"Quite correct," he said.*
> *I replied, "That means we can't be sure about anything."*
> *"Right," he said.*
> *"That means we can't be sure about evolution."*
> *"Oh, no! Evolution is a fact," he blurted out.*
> *He was caught by his own logic. He was demonstrating how his view was determined by his bias.* (Ham, July 1987)

As you can see, this worldview is internally incoherent.

Conversely, the person who believes in God has presuppositions also. They are:

1. God does exist.
2. He originated natural laws.
3. He alone can make or break these laws.
4. He can intervene in nature or choose not to.
5. God is the creator and sustainer of all things.

The benefit of this worldview is that one can fully understand the world around him, including its previous state, its future, destiny, and his place within the scope of humanity. God has created all things, knows everything, and sees past, present, and future simultaneously. He is the One who has revealed the world to us, including humanity's past, present, and future destiny. This is so we may have a full understanding of our world beyond what we can see from our "single moment in time" perspective.

With this as a background, we must look to the one absolute source of truth—the Bible—to provide us with an account of how the universe was made. This source of truth is trustworthy and in all points accurate and true because it was given by God who has been everywhere and seen all things for all time and has infinite knowledge. He alone has a full understanding of the way the universe works. That is, the biblical account is true because it the only account given by the only one who can provide us with absolute truth.

This is further illustrated by the evidence shown in the fine-tuned universe arguments that suggest that the universe is precisely made to the exact specifications for supporting human life. The entropic principle states that hundreds of very specific and exact variables are perfectly configured to allow life on earth—such as the exact rotational axis of the earth, the amount of gravity, and distance from sun. These arguments also suggest that that evolutionary theory is not science but religion based on faith in the atheistic presuppositions of materialism. This explains why there is such a strong, sometimes even hostile, opposition to the teaching that exposes the fatal flaws of evolutionary theory in school classrooms. This is attacking a religion and their foundation belief system. If evolution is not true then there is a creator, one greater than man, who can and has set standards that we must live by. This infringes on the atheist's worldview and restricts him from being able to pursue his own selfish, sensual, and sinful desires that are naturally within all of us. In Isaiah 55:9 God says, "My thoughts are higher than your thoughts and My ways are higher than your ways." To know completely the mind of God would be to make Him in our likeness and bring Him down to our level.

Consider Pascal's wager. The wager is frequently misconstrued and not given the consideration it deserves. It describes a coin-flipping game where you win two cents if its heads and lose only nothing if its tails. Would you play the game? Of course you would. In the long run, you come out ahead. The Wager states the same about belief in God except the odds are even better. If you lose the bet (i.e., there is no God), you lose nothing. If you bet there is a God and you are correct, however, you gain eternal life and are infinitely better than with your possible loss, which would be eternal separation from God in hell.

We follow this wager not just because of eternity, but also because the Christian worldview is the only coherent religion that promises us eternal life. It also brings us the most fulfillment while still here on earth, so we have nothing to lose by following this faith. Paul Little states this well when referring to the Bible. He says:

> *"The Bible has stood the test of critics for 2,000 years. There is not going to be a question that will come up tomorrow that shakes its foundations."* (Little, 1967)

So many people put their faith in evolutionary theory, not because of its overwhelming proof or scientific validity, but because of a pre-commitment to materialism. They hold to it by faith and make it their religion. If we hold evolution up to the light of science and logic we find that it is not scientific or logical at all. As science, it cannot make value judgments. It can only interpret measurable, testable, operable, and repeatable data—and it doesn't omit have such data available.

The answer to the question "How did I get here?" is quite simple. The God of the Bible created us and wants to have a relationship with us. This relationship was broken, however, because of Adam's sin. Romans 5:12 states: "Just as sin entered the world through one man, and death through sin and in this way death came to all men, because all have sinned." This was the consequence of Adam's sin, and as Adam's offspring we have all sinned.

Just as sin entered the world through one man, Adam, so righteousness entered the world through one man, Jesus Christ. Through Christ, God makes a provision for us to overcome the separation from God that sin created. We are also able to have a relationship with God that brings meaning, fulfillment, and joy to our lives both here and for eternity. Those who accept God's way of salvation through His Son Jesus Christ also have the privilege of spending eternity with Him.

WHY IS THERE EVIL AND SUFFERING?

The very concept of "evil" implies a moral law. If we fail to define terms, we may miss the point. The very idea that something we deem "evil" exists assumes there is such a thing as "good." If we do not know what good is then we cannot know what evil is. So when we assume there is evil and good we assume there is a moral law. This moral law is what allows one to judge one deed "good" and another "evil." Further, to assume a moral law assumes a moral lawgiver who establishes the distinction between good and evil; otherwise, good is simply a matter of human personal preference. Thus, evil would be defined merely as something that we would prefer other people not do in order to make our life or our perception of the world around us more comfortable.

Apologist Greg Koukl said this about evil: "Evil is not a created 'thing' but the absence of a thing. Black is not a thing; it is the absence of light. Light is a thing, made up of particles or waves: Same with cold versus hot. They are the absence of the created things. Evil, then, is not a created thing, but the absence of good." (Koukl, n.d.)

Acknowledging the existence of evil leads us to the logical conclusion that if evil exists there must be such a thing as good. If there is such a thing as good than there is a moral law with standards of right and wrong that originate in a source outside of ourselves. If there is a moral law then someone must have given this moral law. This must be true because evil implies a standard above us by which we can judge something to be evil. For instance, if I create a standard and call one thing "right" and another "wrong," why would someone else need to abide by my designated standard? He could just as well create his own standard of right and wrong. Both would have equal weight. So if we believe that evil exists, we admit that there is a transcendent law. If there is a transcendent law, there must be a transcendent lawgiver who set within us standards for distinguishing right and wrong.

Next, we must understand that freedom makes evil possible. From a human perspective, we know that only a preprogrammed robot could live in this moral universe without the possibility of doing evil. Free will—the inherent capacity to choose—enables us to do wrong (i.e., evil). The option of doing right or wrong is with us in every moment. For example, we can choose to do good and tell the truth or we can choose to do evil and tell a lie. Are we always kind and loving to everyone, or do we at times act unkindly or entertain inappropriate or hateful thoughts about our neighbor?

Imagine if we had no such choice but always merely did what was good and right. We would not be free. We would be mere machines, preprogrammed to do right, and what would be lost? A big part of who and what we are. Our ability to choose to love would be lost because a love that is forced is not love. The very emotions and reasoning abilities that enable us to love and do good also enable us to hate and commit evil as well. Thus, our very existence argues for the existence of a supreme being, a moral universe (with standards of right and wrong established by one more powerful than us), and the possibility of evil.

God, our creator, is not powerless with respect to evil, nor does He delight in the evil deeds of His creatures. On the contrary, the evil around us serves another purpose altogether: It points out the goodness of God's holiness and righteousness. Imagine a pitch-black cave hundreds of feet below the ground—utterly dark and devoid of light. What would happen if you lit just one candle in that dark place? It would illuminate the whole cave!

This is how evil (represented by the darkness in the cave analogy) makes God's holiness and character shine so brightly. If there were no evil in this world, His character would not show us so dramatically our need for Him. If there were no evil, we might presume ourselves to be gods. Instead, the evil around us serves to magnify the glory of God and show us our need for Him, both in redemption and in our daily lives.

God also uses evil for His glory by punishing evil deeds, correcting those He loves, and refining the faith of His own children. Each of us has either been spanked by a parent or knows someone who was reared with this type of corporal discipline. Spanking was not to provide the parent pleasure in inflicting pain on the child; rather, it was for correction and was administered out of the parent's love for the child. For example, imagine little Bobby's father catching his son playing out in the street. He warns little Bobby not to play in the street again because he may get hit by a car. Little Bobby hears this warning but decides to ignore it. The next day, when he thinks his father is not watching, he takes his ball out into the middle of the street and begins playing again. His father catches sight of little Bobby and calls the boy inside. The father loves his son dearly and does not want to hurt Bobby. But unfortunately, Bobby has rebelled against his father's warnings and not to act would expose the boy to the risk of much greater injury or even death. His father has a choice to make. He can:

1. Forget about it and not spank Bobby because it would hurt him. However, this would not discourage him from going back out and playing in the street.
2. Spank Bobby for correction, training, and safety. The boy would then be more likely to remember the negative consequences and show how serious the misbehavior was. That would discourage him from playing in the street again.

Which option would be more loving? Option 2, obviously. This is what God does with us. He uses our conscience to correct us and allows evil at times as correction because He loves us and wants to protect us from even worse harm. This caring God has instilled within us a moral compass that looks at this world in its current state and points to something higher and better. It leads us to say, "This isn't the way things are meant to be." We look at the atrocious acts of man and conclude that something has gone badly wrong in our social interactions. We try to explain away this innate sense of morality by ascribing it to social learning, traditions, or conditions placed on us by our parents or culture. Our feelings, though, cannot by themselves give us a true, transcendent ethic or universal moral law. This comes only from someone outside of us, a moral lawgiver, who is God. If we accept a moral law but not a moral lawgiver, we contradict ourselves because they are interdependent. Just as the laws on the books in our state and federal statutes originated with a lawgiver (state and federal legislators), also the moral law originated with a lawgiver.

So when we turn to the condition of suffering in our world, we must address it honestly. Though it is a difficult issue, we must be careful not to close our eyes and shy away from its difficulty and take the easy way out—i.e., by saying there is no God. Without God, there is no reason for suffering. It is a pointless condition of our existence and society. If we are simply accidents in a random universe with not meaning beyond our existence here on earth, then the best remedy for suffering available is more education, more effective social programs, and more self-help books to fix our behavioral problems.

Our problem, however, is not behavioral. It is a problem with the human heart. A world without God is utterly meaningless and leaves us with an empty void and a pointless existence. How would we know what is just, fair, or true unless there were a God who exemplifies all these things in His very character and who, through His word, the Bible, has revealed them to us so we may know them? The fact is, this life is often hard. We do not have to look far to see suffering, starvation, disease, war, famine, and natural disasters. We see this and long for something better, for a reason to get out of bed in the morning. This longing comes from God, the moral lawgiver. He made us for a higher purpose than merely what we see around us in human society.

Many people believe the existence of evil and suffering suggests either that God does not exist or is powerless to stop evil from occurring. This is illustrated in the following traditional logical argument:

>*The Argument* from *Evil*
>
>*(1) If God exists, He is omniscient, omnipotent, and perfectly good.*
>
>*(2) If God were omniscient, omnipotent, and perfectly good, the world would not contain evil.*
>
>*(3) The world contains evil.*

Therefore:

(4) It is not the case that God exists.

This argument displays a serious misunderstanding of the nature of God. The problem comes in premise (2). The person arguing this case misunderstands God's nature and His purpose in creation. God wanted a relationship with us. He created us with the capacity to love Him and know Him intimately. The problem is, we cannot truly love and have a relationship with Him without a free will. A love that is forced is no love at all. Without free will, we cannot have a world of love because there is nothing to compare it to (hate, rejection).

For example, if a teacher instructed you to befriend a student who was different, you had to do it (though, given the choice, you wouldn't have). Regardless of your actions, therefore, you were no true friend. The relationship was forced and there was no true bond, no real friendship. God has the power to stop all evil in this world. It is not a matter of His desire to stop all evil. Instead, He has given us the ability to choose our actions. This free will includes the choice to do either good or evil within His plan for mankind.

- *Premise: Free will requires the potential to do anything one chooses.*
- *Thus, free will requires the potential to do evil.*
- *Conclusion: Thus, removing the potential to do evil would remove free will.*

Other versions of this argument state that if God were truly omniscient, omnipotent, and perfectly good, He would have the ability—and indeed would be required—to stop evil from existing. The person arguing this case simply does not understand how we came to be in this imperfect state. We must consider the causes of evil and why we humans, left to our own desires, would do nothing but evil. God loves us and has established boundaries for our own good. He gave us a choice to do right or wrong (free will). In addition, He gave us a conscience on which He has written the rules of right and wrong. But because of our sinful nature we rebelled against these boundaries.

For example, suppose you are working in a factory and a veteran co-worker comes up to you and says, "Whatever you do, don't press that red button or the ceiling will fall down on you." Then he walks away, leaving you there by yourself. The first thought that crosses your mind is, "I wonder what would happen if I press that red button." This may not have even entered your mind until you were told not to press it. You may never have even noticed the red button until he said something. It is within us to rebel against standards that are set out for our good. We must understand that the evil in this world is a direct result of our sin and rebellion against a holy God. This is not the way God created the world but a perversion of it.

Genesis 3 gives the account of the fall of man. We see that Adam and Eve question God's very goodness. Satan deceived them into thinking that God was "holding out" on them, that there was something better than the garden. They began to suspect that God had not given them everything that was good. So they ate the fruit of the Tree of the Knowledge of Good and Evil to attain this "good" they thought they were missing out on. Unfortunately, this was the first sin, the original source of evil in this world.

Now some of us might be thinking, "This is not fair! Why do I end up with a sinful nature because of someone else's wrong deeds?" The thought process is correct; what we were sentenced to at that moment is known as alien guilt. We have guilt from one man's sin, Adam's. That is the bad news. Romans 5:12 tells us that "sin entered the world through one man, and death through sin, and in this way death came to all men, because all sinned."

Although we may not like the fact that alien guilt is imputed to us, this fact opens the possibility of alien righteousness. Once we understand this righteousness in its fullness, we will love and be thankful for it because it is our only way to salvation from sin. Romans 5:15 continues: "But the gift is not like the trespass. For if the many died by the trespass of the one man, how much more did God's grace and the gift that came by the grace of the one man, Jesus Christ, overflow to the many!"

Christ's substitutionary death on the cross paid the penalty for our sin in full. It took away our guilt, which our own good deeds could never atone for or take away. Finally, Romans 8:1 says, "Therefore, there is now no condemnation for those who are in Christ Jesus, because through Christ Jesus the law of the Spirit of life set me free from the law of sin and death." The good news is that we can be set free from our sinful nature by accepting Christ's payment for our sin, as He is the only One who can make us right with God.

WHAT HAPPENS AFTER DEATH?

According to the Bible, about 4,000 years ago, Job asked this same question. "If a man dies, will he live again?" There are many different views on the afterlife, so let's examine them in context.

EASTERN RELIGIOUS TRADITIONS

Reincarnation is a popular belief among many eastern religions. It basically states that after we die, we live again on earth in another form (perhaps as a tree or a cow). Further, what we do in this life (karma) influences whether we come back in a higher or lower state. Thus, a bad person would come back as something worse whereas a good person would come back as something better. The goal of life is to stop this endless recycling of birth and death. The ultimate achievement is to escape the cycle and become one with the universe or reach a state of nirvana. This back and forth progression is known as the Law of Karma.

There are numerous problems with this view, both logically and practically. First, we see the natural results of this belief system in social structures such as the caste system, where people refuse to help others (especially the "untouchables") because it would interfere with letting them pay for their evil deeds in a past life. This leads to horrific poverty, which is viewed as just deserts for misdeeds done in a past life. These untouchables are consigned to atrocious living conditions in disease-ridden and unsanitary districts. This is attributable directly to a belief system that blames the poor and the unfortunate for their misery.

Second, there is the problem of people's unawareness of their failures from a past life. People cannot remember the past life that reincarnation claims they had. So how could they know the wrong deeds they did and do better?

Third, they must pay a debt for their misdeeds…but there is no creditor to pay. There is no "being" in the reincarnation system to whom one owes a life of good deeds. The only thing close to it would be the ambiguous force called karma.

ISLAM

Islam acknowledges that there is an end of life. Muslims believe the soul is separated from the body by the angel of death—either harshly or painlessly depending on how one has lived. After this, there is an interrogation of the soul by Nakir and Munkar, who ask three questions: "Who is your Lord? Who is your Prophet? What is your religion?"

If all three questions are answered correctly by saying, "Lord is Allah, Muhammad is my prophet, and my religion is Islam," the soul awaits final judgment in peace. If not, the soul awaits final judgment in torment. On the Day of Judgment, one's book of deeds is opened. If one's good deeds outweigh his bad, he goes to heaven. If they do not, he goes to Janah (hell). Heaven is a place full of sensuality. For example, men are rewarded with 72 virgins to fulfill their desires. It is a place of eating, drinking, and happiness. There is no real assurance of salvation given within Islam, except for martyrs.

The underlying problem with Islam's vision of the afterlife is its lack of certainty. One can never be sure which way the scale of good versus bad deeds will tip. Thus, the promise of salvation to martyrs promotes violence—for it is the only assurance one can have of making it to heaven. Thus, Islam leaves all others afraid to die, not knowing if their deeds were good enough to earn their way into heaven. There is no real concept of sin or catalog of wrong deeds other than a list of some injustices that condemn people to Janah. In this religion, man is asked to do good for goodness's sake; evil is permitted as long as the net balance is good. Thus, Islam lacks a source of real justice and a standard to measure what constitutes one "unit" of good and one "unit" of evil.

The individual is left to determine his own scale of good and bad. Death is a dreadful event because there is no God of love or mercy waiting for you, only uncertainty and an arbitrary judge who decides your fate on a whim. People who have no way to be sure of their eternal destiny are typically afraid of death and its inherent uncertainty.

ATHEISM

Finally, let's examine the atheist view of death. This view is, by far, the most simplistic. It states that at death man ceases to exist. A human life is a journey from nothingness to nothingness. Atheists urge us to enjoy life here and now since it is the only life we have—and it is very brief. Atheists often claim that religion makes people look beyond the life we have now. In fact, most of the great humane efforts in human history have been inspired by Christian belief in God (e.g., we minister to the needy and seek to alleviate poverty illness based on our belief in the worth of every human being who is precious in God's sight).

These atheist claims simply ignore the innate human desire to know God and the natural desire to worship something. The atheistic worldview cannot account for these human impulses. Further, atheists are hard-pressed to provide any compelling reason to choose one course of action over another. With no basis for punishment of evil, there is no deterrent to living for your own evil, sensual, and self-centered desires without regard to their consequences on others. Atheism (in its various forms) accounts for why we have a world of people who do not care about their fellow man but live for the moment only. If we fail to keep eternity in sight, we lose our purpose in life and life becomes meaningless.

THE BIBLICAL VIEW

The Bible has answers for the claims of these other religions. It rejects the claim of reincarnation by stating: "…man is destined to die once, and after that to face judgment" (Hebrews 9:27). Dying once refutes the idea that we are in an endless cycle of death and rebirth. Islam claims we are to do good deeds that will earn our salvation. The Bible says this is not possible: "All of us have become like one who is unclean, and all our righteous acts are like filthy rags…" (Isaiah 64:6). This is what God thinks of our good deeds. They are not even considered positive or good things to Him. Our good deeds, in terms of making us righteous, are repulsive to Him. We cannot earn favor with God. He loves us and desires to have a personal relationship with us though the redeeming work of his Son who paid a price for our sins that we could never pay by doing good deeds.

God's justice and righteousness demand that sin be punished. Imagine witnessing the criminal trial of a man accused of a cold-blooded murder. The man is clearly guilty beyond a reasonable doubt, and thus the jury finds him guilty. Suppose at sentencing the presiding judge says, "I have decided to let the defendant go free; no prison time, no probation, no punishment whatsoever. I am sure that he did not mean to harm anyone. He must have simply been having a bad day when this happened." Would you consider this judge a good judge if he let a guilty man go unpunished? Of course not. It is the same way with God. Because of His perfect nature and justice, He cannot let sin go unpunished.

Even more unsettling news is that the Bible declares in Romans 3:23: "... **all** have sinned and fall short of the glory of God." Our good deeds cannot repay our debt of sin. We need God's mercy to save us. There is nothing you or I can do to save ourselves. Given His nature, God must punish sin: "For the wages of sin is death" (Romans 6:23a).

We rest our hope for eternal life on the word of the only One who has died and come back to life. He is the One who can reliably tell us about what happens after death because He has been there and defeated death. So let's see what Jesus had to say about death. Jesus said, "I am the resurrection and the life. He who believes in Me will live, even though he dies; and whoever lives and believes in Me will never die ..." (John 11:25-26a). Jesus clearly claimed that He was the only way to God and through Him alone we can obtain eternal life.

The good news is that "... the gift of God is eternal life through Christ Jesus our Lord" (Romans 6:23b). This is what God freely offers to those who will accept His gift of forgiveness. So what happens after death? Those who accept Christ's gift of salvation will go and be with Him for eternity. Those who reject Him will spend eternity separated from God in hell.

John 3:16-17 sums it up best: "For God so loved the world that He gave His one and only Son, that whoever believes in Him shall not perish but have eternal life. For God did not send His Son into the world to condemn the world, but to save the world through Him." The question is: Are you going to accept Christ's mercy and forgiveness, or are you going to live your life your own way without any regard for Him?

Numbers 21:4-9 illustrates this choice. It tells of a time when the Israelites were complaining against God, claiming that He brought them out of slavery in Egypt only to let them die in the desert. They complained about the food and water God provided as well. The Lord was very angry about this. He allowed venomous snakes to bite the people. Some died and many became sick. So Moses prayed to the Lord and asked for forgiveness on behalf of the Israelites. Moses asked God to take the snakes away. The Lord thus instructed Moses to carve a snake and raise it up on a pole and tell the people that everyone who looked up at the snake would live. Moses did what God asked and told the Israelites what the Lord had said. Everyone who looked at the snake lived, just as the Lord had promised.

We see in this account that the basic human problem—for us and the ancient Israelites alike—is inside us. The poison was inside of the people. They had nothing inside that could save them from the venom of the snakes. We are in the same situation when it comes to our good deeds. We are terminally ill with a disease called sin and will all die. We try to cure ourselves through good deeds. We donate money to a charity or tithe to a church. Or perhaps we abstain from doing "bad" things: We don't drink liquor or use foul language. But…it doesn't cure the sickness we have. We will still die. Nothing inside of us can save us. We need a cure that comes from the outside. Our righteousness is like filthy rags to God. It cannot please Him nor earn His forgiveness. We need a righteousness that comes from outside of ourselves.

Just as Moses made a snake and lifted it up for the Israelites to look to and be saved, we are given Christ who was lifted up not on a pole but on a wooden cross. He was nailed to it so we could have forgiveness for our sins. He was lifted up to die in our place. He is the only medicine that can cure our terminal illness—sin. When we look to Jesus, we can be saved and receive a righteousness that is from outside of us so that when God looks at us, He sees Jesus' perfect righteousness rather than our sin and feeble attempts to be righteous by good deeds. This is our only hope for forgiveness—to look to Him who paid the penalty we all deserved. We can look to Him and live.

CONCLUSION

We have addressed many questions people ask about moral standards, the meaning of life, our purpose, the existence of God, and more. To sum up our answer to these questions, however, we must look to the foundation of truth. What is the foundation of truth? We have already addressed what it is not: It is not our senses or emotions, not our thoughts or even logic, though these are all very useful.

Let's first consider how we prove something is true. We start with something that is "solid" or has a foundation we can trust. We then proceed to use this in proving things that are less certain. For example, we know that $1+1=2$. We use that knowledge to prove things that are less certain, such as solving for the unknown: $1+x=2$. We use what we know about the first equation to determine that x in the second equation equals 1.

We apply the same principle to life. What is the most solid thing on which we can base our view of the universe? Well, a word or manual from the Creator of the universe would be the most trustworthy source, right? God has done this for us. He has given us His Word, which is the most reliable source of truth that exists. A word from God Himself is the most trustworthy source of information of all. God's words come from the Person containing all knowledge, from the One who created the entire universe and its contents and even time itself. Therefore, He comes from a position of knowing all and seeing all. Since God created everything, only He can reveal to us with certainty the inner workings of creation and give us a solid foundation from which to derive knowledge.

Hebrews 6:13 says, "When God made His promise to Abraham, since there was no one greater for Him to swear by, He swore by Himself." A word from God is the highest source of truth man can have. **There is nothing greater we can rely on to prove anything**. Therefore, if we look at God's word, we see God has given mankind a gift of life, which is being created in His image. God gave us the ability to reason. This is the light that God gave to all mankind as described in John chapter 1: *"In the beginning was the Word, and the Word was with God, and the Word was God. He was with God in the beginning. Through Him, all things were made; without Him nothing was made that has been made. In Him was life, and that life was the light of men. The light shines in the darkness, but the darkness has not understood it."*

The same God who created the universe and everything in it is also outside of time, space, and matter. He has been everywhere and seen everything from eternity past. This same God has illuminated us with rationality and has not left us to figure out His existence on our own. He has revealed Himself to us in His word and his creation. Alas, we are without excuse for not worshiping Him and Him alone. God's light shines on us through the world around us, but as sinful people we have rejected this light and prefer our darkness and evil ways. Paul says in Romans 1:18-19: *"The wrath of God is being revealed from heaven against all the godlessness and wickedness of men who suppress the truth by their wickedness, since what may be known about God is plain to them, because God has made it plain to them."*

This wrath is not our version of wrath. It is not a sudden fit of rage or lashing out at others. Rather, it is justified and holy. He has the right and the duty to pour out His wrath against us because our actions are sinful and deserving of death. Not one of us is sinless.

1 John 1:8 says, *"If we claim to be without sin, we deceive ourselves and the truth is not in us."* This godless and wicked state is not limited to certain people. It is the nature state of fallen humanity apart from the redeeming work of Christ. We suppress "the truth." In the Greek, this is in the perfect tense showing **a continuing action** not something we did a long time ago but something we are engaged in on a continuing, moment-by-moment basis, with each wicked thought or action we take. We do this by ignoring our conscience, disregarding God's revelation, refusing to seek Him, and continuing in actions contrary to His moral

instruction in the Bible. God's wrath is for our own good—to turn us to Christ.

Once people understand how hollow sinful pleasure is, their only hope is to cry out for God to save them. This shows that God may be known. He is not silent about Himself or His ways. God is knowable, and information about Him is not hidden. It is not hard to understand and is plain to everyone. God has made it plain to us. This means that those who say they have not read the Bible or that there is a lack of evidence from God are without excuse. God has made what can be known about Himself available to all. He has revealed Himself to everyone without exception, including through creation as we saw in our discussion in the chapter *Is there a God?*

On the other hand, one may ask, "What about people who live in Africa who have never heard the gospel?" Let's first acknowledge that, in our day, we are dealing with a very exceptional case here. Second, let's consider that God not only created us but also placed us within His creation. Psalm 19:1 reveals: "*The heavens declare the glory of God; the skies proclaim the work of His hands.*" As the Bible is God's special revelation of Himself, so the created world is His general revelation of Himself. By denying God's existence, then, man is willfully deceiving himself. Romans 1:20 states: "*For since the creation of the world, God's invisible qualities—his eternal power and divine nature—have been clearly seen, being understood from what has been made, so that men are without excuse.*"

The creation demands the existence of a Creator who designed all the intricate details we observe. The British mathematician Roger Penrose, a close friend of renowned physicist Stephen Hawking, has calculated the probability that chance could account for a universe that could support life as $10^{10^{123}}$ to 1—or 10 followed by 10123 zeros. (Penrose & Denton, 1989; 1998) This general revelation from God, which is revealed to all men, brings them to the point where they can know there is a God. They are then responsible for looking for the God who created the heavens and the earth and search out further specific revelation from Him.

WHAT IS REVEALED IN CREATION?

The creation reveals God's greatness, orderly design, existence, goodness, knowledge, and authority over all things. We also see God's divine nature and eternal power. This is evident in creation itself. The endless expanse of the heavens, the intricacies of the human body, and the complexity of nature with its marvelous design all show how big and powerful God is. How do we observe the world around us? We see it through a proper understanding of scientific discovery, which should lead us to marvel at God's glory, as does our exploration of the other realms of the universe. Because of all of God's glory shown through the universe, we can clearly observe His handiwork.

Being created in God's image, we are without excuse because we see and understand from the things we see around us that God exists. We are totally and completely guilty if we reject the testimony of God's glory in creation's beauty and do not seek Him. Evidence of God's glory is all around us. As science reveals ever more of the intricacies of the world, we should grow in our awareness and awe of God's power. The more we know, however, the more atheistic explanations are proposed to explain away God's role in creation. Why is it that we humans, when confronted by more and more evidence of God's revelation in the created world, are required to create increasingly far-fetched explanations to suppress the knowledge of God? They must actively continue to suppress the truth and explain away God as they discover more of the complexities in our world.

Seeing the wonders of creation and the works of His hands confronts man with the undeniable reality of God's existence. Romans 1:21-23 states: *"For although they knew God, they neither glorified him as God nor gave thanks to him, but their thinking became futile and their foolish hearts were darkened. Although they claimed to be wise, they became fools and exchanged the glory of the immortal God for images made to look like mortal man and birds and animals and reptiles."*

The fundamental problem with man is not that he does not have enough information about God or cannot determine which god is the real god to worship. **His problem is a problem of the will**. If this were not the case, man would not stand before God without excuse. As Jesus said to the Pharisees, *"If you were blind, you would not be guilty of sin; but now that you claim you can see, your guilt remains"* (John 9:41). Here

Jesus was referring to the truth and miracles the Pharisees had witnessed and the scriptures they had read. The Pharisees were the religious leaders of the day. They knew the laws of God better than anyone and yet still failed to see in Jesus the fulfillment of prophecy; they rejected Him and His authoritative teachings. If they had not received the truth (in God's revelation in the scriptures), they would be spiritually blind and thus not guilty. We are not blind either, for God has given us His revelation and, because of this, we can see Him in our surroundings—*if* we are willing to do so. Therefore, our guilt remains if we fail to acknowledge and seek Him.

Man's problem is not so much that he is blind as it is that he turns a blind eye to the clear revelation of God all around him. God is not silent about His existence, nor has He created mankind and left us alone (as the Deists believe). God has provided us with abundant testimony about Himself. We are confronted with God's truth daily, but we do not respond to this truth in the appropriate way—which is to glorify Him and give Him thanks. If we do not glorify and thank Him, our punishment is to become fools as our thinking is darkened. This is the danger in rejecting and suppressing the truth about God: We are left to our own evil thoughts and desires and with nothing to worship but things that have no value. Such things may promise great pleasure or make us feel good temporarily, but in the end, they lead only to emptiness.

As we discussed in chapter *Does absolute truth exist?* all men worship something or someone. The object of their worship is either the God who made us or something lesser than the God who created everything. They worship such things as money, sensuality, success, and other idols of the mind. Romans 1:24-25 states: *"Therefore God gave them over in the sinful desires of their hearts to sexual impurity for the degrading of their bodies with one another. They exchanged the truth of God for a lie, and worshipped and served created things rather than the Creator."*

God leaves those who continually reject the source of truth alone to be subject to their own sinful desires. God does this as a punishment for people who reject Him continually. He allows humans to pursue their evil ways unabated by a conscience. This righteous judgment leaves man to reap the consequences of his sin both on this earth and in eternal separation from God. This is similar to the man who is offered a prime rib dinner (the truth and glory of God) but decides he would rather eat scraps out of a garbage dumpster instead (created things and evil practices).

The consequences of this rejection of God are real. It is not freedom to be released from the restraint of God's gracious hand (any more than it is freedom when a human father lets go of his toddler's hand when walking aside a busy street). Trying to live without God is like a fish trying to live outside of water. The fish is not "finally free" from the restrictions of the fish bowl. He is not free at all; in fact, he is dying in his perceived freedom. God will deal with us in a similar manner if we reject the only source of truth, His Word. God will allow us to experience the consequences of our sin. Sin can be fun for a little while, but *only* for a little while. It comes with a high cost and never delivers on its promises. The goal of this discipline is not merely to punish but to bring a person back to repentance.

The consequences of rejecting God are further described in Romans 1:28-32: *"Furthermore, since they did not think it worthwhile to retain the knowledge of God, He gave them over to a depraved mind, to do what ought not to be done. They have become filled with every kind of wickedness, evil, greed, and depravity. They are full of envy, murder, strife, deceit, and malice. They are gossips, slanderers, God-haters, insolent, arrogant, and boastful; they invent ways of doing evil; they disobey their parents; they are senseless, faithless, heartless, ruthless. Although they know God's righteous decree that those who do such things deserve death, they not only continue to do these very things but also approve of those who practice them."*

In this passage, Paul lists some of the wicked things mankind resorts to when knowingly rejecting God. Even though they know the consequences of their rejection of God lead to death they proceed anyway. Sin always breeds more sin. Notice how the list of wicked things done after the restraining hand of God is removed is *much more vile* than the previous list of wicked things in Romans 1 and 2. When God's restraining hand is lifted, the human mind is darkened and the floodgates of evil and destruction are opened. He is able to participate in evil without feeling shame. Ephesians 4:18-19 states: *"They are darkened in their understanding and separated from the life of God because of the ignorance that is in them due to the hardening of their hearts. Having lost all sensitivity, they have given themselves over to sensuality so as to indulge in every kind of impurity, with a continual lust for more."* Paul clearly shows the downward spiral of God's judgment of those who reject Him while they are still here on earth.

1. Their understanding is darkened.
2. They are separated from God's restraining grace.
3. They harden their hearts.
4. They lose all sensitivity to their conscience.
5. They indulge in sensuality and impurity.
6. They are never satisfied with their current level of wickedness.
7. They long for something more evil to do next.
8. They store up wrath against themselves for the Day of Judgment.

As C. S. Lewis said, "There are only two kinds of people in the end: those who say to God, 'Thy will be done,' and those to whom God says, 'Thy will be done.' All that are in hell chose it." (Lewis C. S., 1946) Given the clear opportunity to choose God, they choose instead the sensuality and worldly pleasures that lead to death.

As I sit here writing this, there is a lump in my throat. Please understand that my intention is not to pass judgment on others or say how bad they are for rejecting God's truth. Each of us are reasonable and will be judged for what we did in regards to God gift of salvation and truth he revealed to us. Once we fully realize how lost we are, being separated from the only One who can give our restless hearts true rest, we must turn from our evil ways and look to the Lord for His free gift of forgiveness. This is not meant to look down on people who are in this state of suppressing God's truth but to gently call them to repentance. It is to plead with them to come back to the One who has left us with so great a witness of Himself in His word to us and in His beautifully crafted creation.

This state of rejection is the sad condition of humanity apart from Christ. People reject God's revelation in creation and in His word. We humans are born sinful and cannot *earn* God's forgiveness under any circumstances. David said in Psalm 51:5, *"I was sinful at birth, sinful from the time my mother conceived me."* Romans 3:10-12 states: *"There is no one righteous, not even one; there is no one who understands, no one who seeks God. All have turned away; they have together become worthless; there is no one who does good, not even one."* Man, left to himself, cannot please God or earn His favor. But the good news is that God is a gracious God.

Jonah said, *"…I knew that you are a gracious and compassionate God, slow to anger, and abounding in love, a God who relents from sending calamity"* (Jonah 4:2b). God is a gracious God who does not want anyone to suffer the eternal consequences of their sin…. But there is a problem. Our sin separates us from a holy God. God cannot simply ignore sin—to do so would violate and contradict His very nature. Sin must be punished, and in His grace God has provided a way to deal with sin through His son Jesus.

To understand God's grace we must understand the differences between three important concepts: justice, mercy, and grace. Let's consider this example. Suppose while driving down the road, you glance in your rearview mirror and see red-and-blue flashing lights behind you. You look down at your speedometer and realize you are traveling 50 miles-per-hour in a 35 mile-per-hour zone. If the policeman gives you a ticket, that would be justice because you are receiving what you deserve. If he merely gives you a warning, that would be mercy. You are not getting what you truly deserve—the ticket. If he writes you a ticket but then says, "I think I'll just keep this and pay it for you," that is grace. Grace is not only not getting what we *do* deserve it is also getting what we do *not* deserve.

God shows us mercy as well. We stand guilty before a holy God for not obeying the laws He gave us. Even one wrong thought, one lie, or even a good thing done for the wrong motive condemns us before a God who demands total perfection. You may be thinking, "Wow, this standard is tough. No one can be perfect!" If that is what you are thinking, you are absolutely correct. No one can meet God's standard of perfection. We all fall short of this standard. Paul put it this way in Romans 3:23: *"For all have sinned, and come short of the glory of God."* God could not just let sin pass without penalty; to do so would be unjust. Any sin, big or small, demands a penalty.

God's word tells us that *"the wages of sin is death"* (Romans 6:23). This is what we earn by our sinful deeds: *death*. Romans 5:8 says, *"But*

God demonstrates His own love for us in this: While we were still sinners, Christ died for us." Christ's death was the only death that could take our place. He is the perfect One who did not deserve the penalty that sin brings. Jesus Christ bore our penalty in our place. We are all sinners in need of God's forgiveness. It is only by God's mercy and grace that we can be saved.

Grace is God's unmerited, undeserved favor toward a person. This grace is made possible only through the sacrifice of the Lord Jesus Christ. Ephesians 2:8-9 says, *"For it is by grace you have been saved, through faith—and this not from yourselves, it is the gift of God— not by works, so that no one can boast."* It was God's work that makes our salvation possible. He imputed (or transferred) our sinfulness onto Christ so that if we merely accept the gift of that sacrifice He will impute (or transfer) Christ's perfect righteousness onto us. Therefore, we are able to stand with confidence before a holy and just God and be accepted on account of His Son's righteousness being put upon us.

My objective in writing this book was to show that you can find the correct answers to life's basic questions. Those answers are found in God's word, the Bible. We can live our lives with a purpose. If you have read this far and do not know what it means to have a personal relationship with Christ, let me encourage you to give your life to Him now. Quit fighting what God has placed in your heart and has made plain to you through His creation. Come and give your life to the only One who is worthy. He is the One who can give your life meaning and purpose. He is the only One who can provide a coherent world and life view. God longs for you to have a relationship with Him in heaven for eternity and has provided us with plenty of evidence that He exists, that He loves us, and that He has a plan for our lives.

APPENDIX

RECOMMENDED READING LIST

The Lie: Evolution by Ken Ham
Why I'm Not an Atheist by Norman Geiler and Frank Turek
Know Why You Believe by Paul Little
An Introduction to Christian Philosophy by Gordon Clark
How Should We Then Live? by Francis Schaffer
Can Man Live without God? by Ravi Zacharias
He is There and He Is Not Silent by Francis Schaffer
A Christian View of Men and Things by Gordon Clark
The God who is There by Francis Schaffer
Jesus Among Other Gods by Ravi Zacharias
Defending the Christian Worldview Against All Opposition by Greg Bahnsen

LECTURES:

The Great Debate: Does God Exist? Between Greg Bahnsen and Gordon Stein

BIBLIOGRAPHY

Bahnsen, G. L. (March 2007). *Pushing the antithesis: the apologetic methodology of Greg L. Bahnsen* . Powder Springs, Georgia: American Vision, Inc.

Carnegie, A. (1913-1918). (Unknown, Interviewer)

Dictionary, W. (n.d.). Retrieved from http://www.merriam-webster.com/dictionary/science

Faith, T. W. (n.d.). *Creeds.net*. Retrieved 1996, from Creeds.net: http://www.creeds.net/Westminster/shorter_catechism.html

Geehan, E. (1971). *Jerusalem and Athens: Critical Discussions on the Theology and*. Phillipsburg, NJ: P&R Publishing.

Ham, K. (July 1987). *The Lie: Evolution*. Master Books.

Hippo, S. A. (AD 397-398). *Confessions of St. Augustine*. Roman Africa Province.

Kansas. (1978). *Dust in the Wind*. Topeka, KS: Don Kirshner's Music Organization .

Koukl, G. (n.d.). *Stand to Reason*. Retrieved from http://www.str.org/site/News2?page=NewsArticle&id=8039

Lewis, C. S. (1952). *Mere Christianity*. New York, NY: HarperCollins Publishers Inc.

Lewis, C. S. (1946). *The Great Divorce*. New York: HarperCollins Publishers.

Little, P. (1967-01-19). *Know why you believe*. Colorado Springs: Scripture Press Publications, Inc. (PWH).

Loveshade, R. (2010, 8 6). *Five Blind Men and an Elephant*. Retrieved from http://discordia.loveshade.org/apocrypha/elephant.html

Penrose, R., & Denton, M. (1989; 1998). *The Emperor's New Mind; Nature's Destiny*. New York: The New York: The Free Press.

Prager, D. (1992). Liberalism and the Los Angelos Riots. *Ultimate Issues*.

Unfred, D. (March 1982). *Evolution as religion*.

Zacharias', R. (1994). *"Can Man Live Without God?"*. Nashville, TN: W Publishing Group.

Zacharias, R. (2000). *Jesus Among Other Gods*. Nashville, TN: W Publishing Group.

ABOUT THE AUTHOR

Paul Elwell is a doctoral student who lives in Mattawan, Michigan with his wife, son as well as two golden retrievers. Paul enjoys studying philosophy and theology and this book is the result of his personal study.

INDEX

Please write me with your comments or questions related to this book at:

Paul Elwell
Po Box 383
Mattawan, MI 49071